THE BENEFITS OF MARIJUANA

Physical, Psychological and Spiritual

by
Joan Bello

LIFESERVICES PRESS
SUSQUEHANNA, PENNSYLVANIA

THE BENEFITS OF MARIJUANA:

Physical, Psychological and Spiritual

Published by LIFESERVICES PRESS
POST OFFICE BOX 61
SUSQUEHANNA, PENNSYLVANIA 18465

www.benefitsofmarijuana.com

FINAL EDITION
Library of Congress Catalogue Card Number: 97-92699
ISBN 978-0-9660988-2-2
Printed in the U.S.A.

Acknowledgments

Invaluable contributions to this work were made by my loving husband, Andrew Bello, who spent many long evenings with me as we labored over this book to complete it. His relentless support, constant encouragement, and many suggestions gave us both the strength to continue during the most difficult time of our lives.

The conscientious expertise and patience of Barbra Haynes in preparing this manuscript cannot be measured, except to say that her effort was surely beyond the call of duty, even for a daughter.

The Final Version of this book represents the professional touch of Tanya Goodroad who spent many hectic hours formatting, editing, adding to and perfecting the text. I am ever grateful for her superior competence in the midst of confusion.

Special thanks to Steve Willis for the front cover which portrays what this book needs 500,000 words to say.

I need to thank my father, who supported my work wholeheartedly even before he understood its righteousness. He has been the most alert, gentle and steadfast influence of my entire life.

The ultimate inspiration for this work, however, along with the intuitive understanding as to how and why to proceed is without question due to the guidance granted me by the mind and heart expansion of the marijuana plant.

TABLE OF CONTENTS

The Cover

Cover representation of the Caduceus, signifies the Hindu understanding of human life, most extensively explained and emphasized in the esoteric science of Kundalini Yoga. The body is energized through two invisible passageways that run on either side of the equally invisible Main Energetic Channel (Sushuma). All three of these paths follow the human spine from base to head. At the bottom of Sushuma is the latent power of pure consciousness. It is usually depicted as a sleeping serpent, lying dormant throughout the lives of almost all people. Igniting this power fulfills the ultimate goal of life; to raise the individual consciousness to the point of Non-Duality. Ida is on the left side of Sushuma. It is associated with moon power, coolness, the feminine, the negative and the mysterious. Pingala is on the right side. It is red, hot, masculine and related to the energy of the sun. Their division is the dualism of limited consciousness. Perfect balance between these two opposing and divided energies is enlightenment or the highest consciousness. The opposing energies run through the single central channel, thereby allowing the subject to experience the wonder of undifferentiated consciousness. This is the subjective and mystical experience of the resolution of the opposites, which is attended by perfect evenness in the flow of the breath, singularity of mental focus, joy and compassion.

It is no coincidence that in the human body, running alongside the spinal column, are the Sympathetic and Para-Sympathetic nerve chains that cause opposite activities of excitement and relaxation of the Autonomic Nervous System. This two-fold system is the physical counterpart of the more subtle energetic paths of Ida and Pingala. When there is perfect balance between the two sides of the Autonomic Nervous System, the alert relaxation of higher consciousness is the result.

Marijuana balances the Autonomic Nervous System - which is the counterpart of balancing the more subtle energies of Ida and Pingala. Marijuana expands the power of the breath, enhances the power of the mind, imparts a sense of well-being and encourages peace and kindness.

PREFACE: A Letter From Jail
Dale R. Gowin

Children of a future age
Reading this indignant page,
Know that in a former time
Love! Sweet Love! Was thought a crime.
--- William Blake

It is a great honor and privilege to introduce to the world Joan Bello's courageous and insightful treatise on the Benefits of Marijuana. Grounded in multidisciplinary science and bolstered by a wealth of documentation, this groundbreaking work provides ample evidence to support the intuitive knowledge of millions, that Cannabis offers healing potentials for the human body, mind and spirit.

For too long, the many millions who have known this truth have cowered in fear beneath the shadows of deception and repression. In our own lives we have borne witness to the healing virtues and spiritual gifts bestowed by Nature through this plant, yet we have languished timidly as our liberty to pursue this happiness was stripped away; and we have watched in silence as our sisters and brothers were hauled away, their homes and property seized, for no crime other than peacefully partaking of, and sharing, the spirit-nurturing Light that is crystallized within the cells of this verdant and virtuous vegetable. No longer can we abide in this conspiracy of silence. The clarion call of Truth rings from these pages. An answering echo is the ancient promise of prophecy: The truth will set you free.

My relationship with Cannabis began in 1967, when I was 17 years old. I discovered, to my amazement and delight that this humble plant had the power to bestow the gift of Divine Grace to one who would respectfully partake of its resinous flowers and leaves. Its subtle magic gently lifted me from the doldrums of daily life, into realms of deeply enriched clarity of mind and vibrancy of vision. I gradually came to realize that the miraculous gift of consciousness enhancement granted by Cannabis and the other psychedelic plants was the most valid, genuine, and authentic manifestation of Spiritual Light that I had ever encountered. Now, after 30 years largely devoted to the Spiritual Quest, this realization remains undimmed.

Ten years after first partaking of the holy Herb, I crossed the Rubicon of personal commitment and devoted myself to public activism against prohibition while serving a 12-year prison sentence.

My research about the Holy Herb led to some truly amazing discoveries. Among the things I learned were these:

Cannabis (marijuana) was probably the first plant ever cultivated by humans. In the Neolithic period, as the glaciers of the Pleistocene ice age were receding from Earth's temperate zones, nomadic food gatherers collected Cannabis along with other wild plants. Its fertile seeds, a protein-rich food source, sprouted readily and grew abundantly in the disturbed soil near their campsites. The prevalence of the plant near Neolithic campsites and its ease of cultivation spurred the transition from a nomadic food-gathering economy to settled agriculture – a quantum leap in the evolution of human civilization.

Cannabis was a uniquely useful survival resource to our prehistoric ancestors. Every part of the plant had important uses. Fibers stripped from the stalks were twisted into twine for bows, fishing lines and snares, and were woven into fabric for clothing and canvas for shelter. The wood-like "hurds" inside the stalks were used as cooking and heating fuel. The seed, as well as providing sustaining food, was pressed for oil, providing light in our earliest earthenware lamps and pushing back the threatening shadows of night. The leaves and flowers were used as medicine – Cannabis is mentioned in the earliest extant herbals – and were used by shamans and worshipers as aids to spiritual revelation.

In more recent eras, the Cannabis plant was used extensively industry for the manufacture of paper, plastics, fabrics, fuels, chemicals, cosmetics, and literally thousands of other products. It was the economic value of these applications – and its competitive threat to the monopoly profits of petroleum-based corporate cartels – that led to the imposition of Cannabis prohibition in the 20th century.

Cannabis was widely respected as a medicine since ancient times throughout the world. Before prohibition, the U.S. Pharmacopoeia listed over 100 approved uses for it, and it was one of America's most popular over-the-counter medications in the 19th century. Cannabis was the standard treatment for asthma, emphysema, epilepsy, migraine, arthritis, glaucoma, insomnia, and many other conditions. Recent research has shown that Cannabis is a safer and more effective treatment for many of these conditions than the expensive synthetic pharmaceuticals preferred by the monopoly-based medical establishment.

Cannabis has been recognized as a spiritual sacrament by virtually every religious tradition in the world. Chinese Taoists, Hindus from India, Tibetan Buddhists, the Gnostics, and Essenes of Judaism, Coptic Christianity, the Sufi and Ishmaili traditions of Islam – all of these and more have known and respected the holiness and religious value of the Cannabis experience.

There is no truth to the government-sponsored propaganda about the alleged dangers of marijuana. From the "reefer madness" campaign of the 1930s to the claims made by DARE and the Partnership for a Drug Free America today, the prohibitionist rhetoric is nothing more than a smokescreen of lies and fabrications, promulgated by the Corporate-Monopoly State for economic and political purposes. Every unbiased scientific study has found that Cannabis is non-addictive, non-toxic, and potentially beneficial.

Joan Bello's illuminating text acknowledges the truth about Cannabis without kowtowing to the sacred cows of prohibitionist political correctness, and pushes the debate past conventional limits, into virgin territory fraught with relevance to today's most urgent social issues. A work of 21st-century science, this book sets the agenda for a new generation of discourse. The bold thesis presented in these pages is that Cannabis is not only harmless and benign as a recreational euphoriant, but also a holistic medicine for deep healing of the human body, mind and spirit – and a specific remedy for the spiritual malaise of Western Civilization, the disastrous disharmony that characterizes the last decade of the Old Millennium. Cannabis played a vital role in human evolution thousands of years ago, providing sustenance and solace to the scattered survivors of the great glaciers. It may yet prove to be an equally important asset in our next great evolutionary hurdle as the human race faces the challenge of survival into the New Millennium.

As this book makes clear, Cannabis is an essential part of the natural birthright of all Earth-dwellers, and its prohibition is truly a crime against humanity.

Dale R. Gowin, #91-B-0209
Midstate Correctional Facility
Marcy, New York
July 4, 1996

From the author,

In 1986, when I began writing The Benefits of Marijuana, the idea of physical or psychological benefits coming from this much maligned illegal plant was outlandish. But my own experience with marijuana had given me an intuitive, unshakeable recognition of its wonder. In addition to being forever grateful for the *marijuana consciousness*, conventional medicine had failed my 11 year old epileptic son who was miraculously improved with marijuana. My husband and I could and did spend hours just talking, listening to music, or reading to each other with the gentle lift of grass. Meditation was fuller, concepts clearer, even nature was more beautiful. I was more relaxed, more assured and less angry. And my spirituality was awakened!

The Eastern Studies Master of Science Program that I completed under the tutelage of an accomplished Yogi was an intense and inspired transmission of esoteric knowledge and its physical and psychological validation in Western science. The concentration necessary to complete the program with the constant companion of grass, transformed me.

While enrolled in the rigorous curriculum, I amassed an incredible library concerning marijuana – its history, its politics, its sacramental heritage, the science behind its effects, and its medical applications. The Benefits of Marijuana was the result of this research.

More than twenty years later, it is no longer outlandish to discuss the benefits of marijuana. It seems with every passing day, a new study validates the old tradition. But the fact that marijuana balances the Autonomic Nervous System, which is the yogic goal for health and spiritual accomplishment, has not changed. Whereas this book presents the overall balancing mechanism of Marijuana Therapy, not until the 21rst Century has science confirmed with supreme precision the boundless wonders of this ancient gift of nature. With the last edition of this book, I have included timely and specific medical applications of marijuana and have tried to impart the need for the *marijuana consciousness* in modern living.

August 12, 2007

Introduction

This book has gone through many printings. Originally, *The Benefits of Marijuana* was begun as a personal research project because I wanted to understand the process by which this plant enhanced my consciousness. There was no problem in discovering the historical utilizations of hemp/marijuana for fuel, fiber, food, medicine and even religious sacrament. I found numerous philosophical essays exalting *"marijuana consciousness."* But nowhere could I find a satisfactory discussion that explained by what physical mechanism the Cannabis Sativa plant gave extra depth to my perceptions. And, although I discovered references to specific maladies for which Cannabis, in years past, was said to offer relief, no definitive scientific reason for its healing ability seemed to exist. While tests that proved its complete safety were in abundance, and ancient tomes spoke of it as a sacred "gift from the gods," in the modern literature, Cannabis was portrayed as a very dangerous drug. It all added up to a mystery I needed to solve.

Meanwhile, national awareness concerning the issue of Cannabis as medicine barely existed. The criminalization of recreational marijuana verses the right of adults to choose their own vice was the popular controversy. Although many sick people were employing Cannabis to relieve their symptoms, they were isolated from each other and silent about their need, purchasing pot on the black market when it was available and affordable. Some patients chose to grow their own, and many of those patients were arrested and imprisoned.

In the 70s and 80s thousands (perhaps millions) of seriously sick people did not have any idea that marijuana could lend relief from their disease, and possibly offer a turning toward healing, if not physically, at least by unhinging them from the mental stress that exacerbates so many illnesses. Many of the patients, who enjoyed Cannabis regularly, to feel and function better harbored guilt over their use. Their personal experience contradicted everything they had been taught to believe. They were confused and did not understand how such a maligned substance could so enhance their well being. I wrote this book because, after years of documented research, and through personal experience and formal training, I had come to understand the astonishingly simple mechanism by which marijuana benefits the physical, psychological and, in some cases, even the spiritual elements of human life. I was committed to sharing that knowledge.

Since I first started working on this project, there have been great strides in the hemp/marijuana/Cannabis movement. In the early nineties, a synchronous realization in the world of *marijuana consciousness* emerged concerning the benefits that this plant offers, and the importance of making this information available to the public. This realization grew to a crescendo (among people, who were otherwise completely unconnected) in response to any number of conjuncting factors. One of the earliest visible influences was Jack Herer's exposé, *The Emperor Wears No Clothes*, documenting that hemp has an almost boundless potential for replacing environmentally devastating industries. We can stop cutting forests down for paper, and instead grow hemp - without pesticides and without fertilizers. We can stop burning fossil fuels which poison our atmosphere, and instead grow hemp for biodegradable fuel. We can replace cotton, which entails using poisonous fertilizers and pesticides, we don't need synthetics manufactured from petrochemicals - we can just grow hemp. Neither do we need any petro-chemicals for paints, or lumber from trees for building boards - all were demonstrated to be perfectly feasible utilizations of Hemp in Herer's revolutionary work. As word spread, lists of specific diseases that could be medicated with Cannabis (which actually had been medicated with Cannabis for thousands of years) became well known. Medicine that comforts, aids, strengthens and clarifies is the history and the potential of this outlawed plant. The situation for many patients, once exposed to Herer's information, became one in which they realized that they were, first of all, not alone, and secondly, not mistaken concerning their personal experience. Their intuition was validated. Hemp / Cannabis / Marijuana made them feel good because it has very individual and measurable remedial effects for a number of diverse health problems.

With the birth of the Internet, the hemp/marijuana patients and advocates were no longer isolated or in the dark. The information on Cannabis Sativa was limitless. There is no question that the technological wonder tool of the internet has made all the difference. With both knowledge and unity, the move toward demanding recognition for marijuana as medicine has been energized.

Dr. Lester Grinspoon, the Harvard psychiatrist/professor who has been an advocate for marijuana, since he first started his studies on the plant, back in the 70's has published moving testimonials from marijuana patients that have made a deep impact in the conventional field of medicine. Owing largely to his efforts, the *New England Journal of Medicine* expressed its support for medical marijuana in January, 1997: "I believe that a federal policy that prohibits physicians from alleviating suffering by prescribing marijuana for seriously ill patients is misguided, heavy-handed, and inhumane. Some physicians will have the courage to challenge the continued proscription of marijuana for the sick. Eventually, their actions will force the courts to adjudicate between the rights of those at death's door and the absolute power of bureaucrats whose decisions are based more on reflexive ideology and political correctness than on compassion." (J.P. Kassirer)

Grinspoon's book, *Marihuana: The Forbidden Medicine*, gives in-depth testimony from patients for whom Cannabis represented their only effective and safe medicine. Over the years, his stance has become bold, until he finally called marijuana -"the wonder drug of the century." He further endeared himself to all marijuana proponents, when he publicly acknowledged his personal use and admiration for Cannabis as an enhancement to his own life experience.

In the 80s, the U.S. government actually recognized Cannabis as medicine with the "Compassionate Protocol" for patients whose diseases responded only to intact marijuana. This program was a well-kept secret for years with only 10 or so patients. In 1992 word leaked out. Hundreds of AIDs victims signed up for medical marijuana. The government closed the program with no notice! The Class Action Lawsuit for Cannabis Therapeutics in 1999 actually grew out of this incredibly calloused termination. It was an attempt to gain the same constitutional rights for all citizens who need medical marijuana (as those patients who were receiving 300 marijuana cigarettes a month from the government since the beginning of the program in 1978). The Class Action Lawsuit was dismissed on the technicality that - there was closed discussion among committee members before closing the program to new patients. Therefore, (because they discussed it) it was deemed legal that only a few patients receive the medicine they need while the rest of the patients in the country would not. The Compassionate Protocol has continued throughout the last decades for those few "special" patients. In 2007, five of these patients are still living. They are still supplied with University of Mississippi-grown U.S. Government Cannabis.

While efforts to educate the general public as to the boundless medical applications of Cannabis were growing exponentially, strong resistance was building on the other side. We can never discount the fear that the *marijuana mindset* portends for a competitive-driven society. Marijuana is known to alter focus from a materialistic ethic to one of compassion and timeless values. It enhances tolerance and cooperation in direct opposition to the militaristic mentality of acquisition and domination, and consequently is a direct threat to the reigning economic system and political establishment.

Despite the "War on Drugs" mentality - constantly fueled with fear and misinformation, the voters of California and Arizona perceived the truth about Cannabis as medicine and responded. Proposition 215 was a grass-roots movement that went directly to the people in 1996. It was a historical moment when the Compassionate Use Proposition was passed. Doctors in California were given the right (by the state) to recommend Cannabis for severe discomforts and diseases. In Arizona, Proposition 200 followed suit. The last decade has demonstrated that the public understands the needs of marijuana patients. Referendums of the people and some enlightened legislatures are allowing medical marijuana in contradiction to the federal government. It is only a matter of time, when enough states (2/3 of them) will authorize marijuana as medicine. Then the U.S. government must accede (by law) to the wishes of the majority of its citizens. But, meanwhile, patients in dire need of Cannabis will continue to suffer in silence, buy on the illegal market, grow in secret, relocate to another state or even a different country, or perhaps, unfortunately, be targeted as criminals and imprisoned. By no means is the political struggle over.

Doctors considering recommending medical marijuana, even though in line with state law and authorized by a direct vote of the people, were threatened by the government with Federal prosecution As a result of this threat, doctors-in-good-standing and documented marijuana patients filed a Federal Lawsuit challenging the constitutionality of such an intrusion into the patient/doctor confidentiality. The doctors and the patients won! By the turn of the century, marijuana as medicine had become a reality.

But modern history of marijuana prohibition has had many moments of encouragement and many more set-backs. In 1944, the LaGuardia Committee discredited all reasons for outlawing hemp/marijuana:

> The lessening of inhibitions and repressions, the euphoric state, the feeling of adequacy, the freer expression of thoughts and Ideas, and the increase in appetite for food, brought about with hemp/ marijuana suggests therapeutic possibilities. (Chairman, G. Wallace)

Then again, in 1988, Court Hearings were held to determine if marijuana had any medicinal value. The DEA's own Law Judge, Francis Young gave his famous decree after in-depth research of two years:

> "By any measure of rational analysis, marijuana can safely be used within a supervised routine of medical care.... marijuana is one of the safest therapeutically active substances known to man."

The truth was ignored then, as it still is now (2007). The DEA Administration maintains marijuana in a Schedule I status: "Dangerous, with no medical value." That categorization has been challenged in the courts too often to count and every angle has been presented to no avail.

The right of citizens to use marijuana has actually become widespread around the world, but global changes in international law have hardly been reported here in the U.S. In Columbia, it is legal to possess up to one ounce for personal pleasure. On the other side of the earth, in Germany, Switzerland, and the Netherlands, almost in time-sync with the Colombian about-face, it became legal to possess up to one ounce. In addition, medical marijuana is recognized in most of the industrialized nations. Motivation for these major changes in so many nations came about through the explosive populations of minor drug-charged inmates in the prison system. The drain to fragile economies was more important than the disfavor of the American government. The world is likewise embracing the hemp/marijuana plant for its many varied uses in industry. Hemp is actually becoming a major crop once again - in all but America.

Switzerland and Holland both grow and distribute "medical grade" hemp. In Belgium, Canada, France, Luxembourg, Netherlands, Portugal, Italy, Germany and the United Kingdom, Cannabis Laws have been relaxed or even allow medical marijuana. World-wide, scientists are conducting tests to understand the specific benefits of marijuana for a wide array of disease. In the U.S., the prestigious Institute of Medicine has acknowledged that marijuana is not a "gateway" to drugs, and that "withdrawal" and "tolerance" is not part of the marijuana profile.

If the end results of this campaign against marijuana were not destructive for the earth and fraught with pain and suffering for so many people and animals, we could almost laugh at the foolishness. Here is a plant that grows everywhere with ease, that can underwrite the commercial needs of the globe without pesticides, harmful fertilizers or mega-machines and without destroying the atmosphere or life forms of the planet, which was always a medicine as far back as humans kept records (and before that). It eases instability of the human organism, with utmost safety!

In the first analysis, the main opposition to marijuana seems to be authoritarian folly. The same government that distributes marijuana to a special few seems to have no logic behind its public stance against marijuana. On closer observation, however, it becomes obvious that an enormous loss of power would occur to the multinational drug companies if marijuana's limitless medical possibilities were unleashed, not to mention the loss of profit and power of the industrial giants, such as logging companies, oil companies, cotton farmers and manufacturers should marijuana/hemp products flood the markets. Freedom for Cannabis represents great loss to the booming prison/legal industry, as well and most significantly, to the Black Market traders who wield their control behind the scenes. Despite underhanded tactics to discredit marijuana, and to maintain prohibition regardless of the cost to taxpayers or the suffering of patients or the anguish of families destroyed by the penal system, advocates for freedom for Cannabis continue to push forward. Intensive research of whole plant medical applications is now being developed throughout the world. (Not in the U.S.)

For me, every year that passes demonstrates a further progression in understanding the wonders of marijuana. Up until now, this book represented technical study, including all kinds of academic research. It was framed under my own holistic orientation, taking into account observations and experience of many years, as well as self-study. However, in no way was I prepared for what I learned first-hand - from the patients. Nothing I read, imagined, or wrote was as shocking as the absolute savior-like effects of marijuana on the hundreds of seriously ill patients whom I was honored to interview and grew to know while working as Director of the People's Lawsuit for Therapeutic Cannabis.

When I first put forth the hypothesis that marijuana balanced the Autonomic Nervous System, from which all kinds of health benefits accrue - there were no people to validate this reasoning, and of course, absolutely no science. With the publication of the revised edition of The Benefits of Marijuana, I was able to include some of the Class Action Patients' summaries and astounding relief that Cannabis affords. In addition, the final edition of this work is witness to hundreds of serious scientific studies that prove the specific as well as the general benefits of marijuana for body, mind and spirit.

Chapter 1 • The Effect of Marijuana
Classification of Marijuana

It is little wonder that the unique makeup of marijuana has caused major confusion over its effects on the human body.. Neither a stimulant nor depressant, pharmacologically it is classified by itself (Weil; Schultes and Hofmann). That it produces changes in mood has allowed for its classification as a hallucinogen, but this definition is ultimately unsatisfactory, since hallucinogens are chemically unrelated to the molecular makeup of marijuana. Plant hallucinogens and hormones manufactured in the brain are both water soluble. They both contain nitrogen and are categorized therefore as alkaloids. But the marijuana plant has no nitrogen, and its active principles occur in resinous oil - not released in water.

> Almost all plants that alter consciousness contain the element nitrogen and therefore belong to the large class of chemical compounds known as alkaloids. Among the more important plants with psychoactive properties, only Hemp/Marijuana has active principles which do not contain nitrogen. (Shultes and Hoffman)

The alteration in mental processes that takes place with hallucinogens occurs because of their similarity to brain hormones. The usual pathways of neuronal messages within the brain change dramatically and directly when hallucinogens are introduced. But marijuana does not affect this mechanism at all. Instead its effects on brain patterns are indirect and are mediated through the more subtle regulation of the Autonomic Nervous System (ANS) as will be explained in the following pages.

To classify marijuana as a drug ignores both its physiological effects and its chemical makeup. The term "drug" connotes concentration of a substance to its most powerful form, but marijuana is unprocessed, dried vegetation from a strong smelling annual herb called Cannabis. It maintains its natural complex chemistry of both active and inactive compounds rather than concentration of a single compound.

> The relationships people form with plants are different from those they form with white powders...users tend to stay in better relationships with them over time. One reason for this difference is that plants are dilute preparations, since the active principles are combined with inert vegetable matter...Doctors and pharmacologists refer to these predominating chemicals as the active principles of

the plants, which would be fine except that it implies all the other
constituents are inactive and unimportant. (Weil and Rose)

The main problem with drugs is their danger, since all drugs are
defined as poisonous, depending upon dose, which means overdose can
cause death. However, marijuana has no known level of toxicity. The
amount needed to produce a lethal reaction has been estimated at from
eating five pounds at one time, to smoking 40,000 joints in one day, far
beyond any physical possibility (NORML). "It does not kill people in
overdose or produce other symptoms of obvious toxicity."

The term "narcotic" describes a drug or poison that reduces sensibility
by depressing brain function, which can cause death by stopping
respiration. Because marijuana has none of these effects, its legal
classification as a narcotic is completely without basis. "Guided by
the...Victorian ethic, the U.S...easily made the mistake of classifying
marijuana as a narcotic. In point of fact, it is a mild euphoriant."
(Editor's note in the 1973 re-publication of Mayor's Committee, NYC)

Since marijuana contains nearly 500 complex molecules, all attempts
to understand how it works by the usual modern method of isolating each
part and testing its effects have failed. Because of these failures, many
grave misconceptions have developed, "its effects are hard to describe
because they are so variable" (Weil and Rosen).

Scientific and Scholarly Studies

Over the last century, published scientific investigations conducted by
the governments of India, Costa Rica, Jamaica, Greece, Canada, the U.S.
and the City of New York have all concluded that marijuana is not only
the safest recreationally used substance, but also has unmistakably
unique therapeutic properties. Since the 1960s marijuana has been the
subject of thousands of studies by the U.S. Government, pharmaceutical
companies, and private agencies. Even though the investigations funded
by the government and pharmaceutical companies set out specifically to
prove the harmfulness of marijuana, the evidence was quite the contrary.
Time and again untested and preposterous allegations have been
highlighted in the press, such as, marijuana causes birth defects, brain
damage, lung cancer and even sterility. However, these accusations have
been scrutinized and proven untrue. The favorable results of the
government-sponsored investigation begun during Nixon, was released
during Carter's term. Marijuana was almost decriminalized at that time

because the Commission could find no danger whatsoever issuing from its use, either for health or behavior. Owing to fierce political pressures from the hard-core conservative elements, however, marijuana remained stigmatized and illegal, and its prohibition is a continuing saga.

It should be noted that in 1996, the American Medical Association was about to declare publicly in favor of legalizing marijuana at one of its symposiums. This was, however, nipped in the bud in the nick of time because of pressure from the conservative element within the organization and the government. The declaration of support for the medical value of marijuana was nearly taken because of the increasing number of therapeutic benefits for which marijuana could no longer be ignored: AIDS-related symptoms, asthma, chemotherapy-caused nausea, glaucoma, spasticity, phantom pain, emphysema, epilepsy, stress and loss of appetite. The extent of these applications (for which marijuana's benefits are/were well known) points unmistakably to a dramatic healing effect of the entire organism. Nevertheless, what was clear and obvious was denied. Many of the private studies (before the ban on marijuana research in '72) presented a wealth of information, indicating possible medical / psychiatric applications, but these findings were not integrated into a general holistic understanding. Over time, the results were forgotten. Since then studies with marijuana (exempted from the government ban) have been undertaken only by pharmaceutical companies. Their goal is to manufacture a synthetic compound that will fill the needs of the patients while also fulfilling the requirements of being patented for profit.

To be understood fully, marijuana's effects must be viewed holistically. The complexity of action of the 460+ known chemicals cannot be divided and then explained as the product of the total response. While one cannabinoid compound acts in one direction, yet another moderates the first, and so on down the line, perhaps close to 500 times. Only complete consideration of the innumerable elements (both active and inactive) will serve up the reality of their total effect. And only by observation of the total reaction within the body and on the person can we begin to clear up the confusion about the effect of Cannabis on the human body. To understand this action, we need to understand the Autonomic Nervous System.

Autonomic Nervous System

The Autonomic Nervous System (ANS) might well be called the Eighth Wonder of the World. Our heart beat, our breath, our temperature, our appetites, all our cellular exchanges are regulated by this automatic pilot. It sends the right signal, to the right organ, at the right time - without conscious knowledge or effort. The primary control center is the hypothalamus (section of the brain), which activates automatic processes in accordance with the body's needs at any moment.

Marijuana (comprising various cannabinoid compounds) molecules fit "pharmacologically distinct receptors" in this complicated mechanism.

> The key to understanding how the brain communicates through this array of chemical messages lies in the shape of the chemicals and their receptors. Distributed throughout the body on the surface of cell membranes are hundreds, perhaps thousands of different types of molecular structures called receptors. Each type of receptor has a characteristic 3-dimensional shape and, like a lock, can only be opened or activated by a chemical key with the correct corresponding shape. This cellular selectivity provides evidence for the existence of specific receptors for the cannabinoids...The hypothesis can be proposed for a 'cannabinoid' receptor and findings...suggest (the existence of)...a pharmacologically distinct receptor." (Ornstein/ Sobel & Howlett)

This "fit" has led to much speculation in the scientific community concerning the ancient evolutionary connection between the marijuana plant and human ancestry. Scientists have discovered that there is a brain hormone - keyed to this receptor (Devane; Mechoulam). Preliminary testing has demonstrated its identical effects with the THC molecule. This "new" brain chemical (which unlocks the same receptor as THC) clarifies that effects of the cannabinoids are completely compatible with human organisms. Our own brain produces "Anandamide," appropriately named after the Indian word for "bliss." What is truly amazing is that the natural chemical is a completely different shape than the cannabinoid molecule, suggesting a subtle, electromagnetic twin charge between the plant compound and the brain hormone, not yet detectable.

The ANS operates through two branches, the Sympathetic and the Parasympathetic, each exerting its opposing influence in constant complex chemical cooperation to balance the body (homeostasis) under all conditions. The ANS is made up of chains of two kinds of neurons that travel from the brain and spinal column to organs throughout the body. Increasing Sympathetic activity results in outpourings of the body's chemical-stimulants, whereas increase in Parasympathetic action is accommodated by the body's chemical depressants.

The ANS is intimately connected to the mind so that when we interpret our situation as safe, when we are not tired or worried, our autonomic system rests at equilibrium, eliciting neither additional excitation (stimulating chemicals) nor relaxation (depressing chemicals). If this mode of balance were maintained, psychosomatic illnesses would not exist. But life poses a complicated array of continual dilemmas, and naturally we react. Because the way we feel reflects and is reflected by our body chemicals, we need not ingest any substance from outside our organisms to change our moods. Instead through the autopilot of the ANS, body hormones are called forth by the situations we find ourselves in (such as rush hour traffic) and by various forms of recreation (TV programs), and most significantly by how we perceive and think. Modern habits of excess result in imbalance - we work too hard, we think too much, we overeat, we over sleep - the net effect of which taxes our ability to maintain equilibrium. When an overabundance of excitement occurs in one moment, the ANS eventually compensates by equalizing doses of depressant hormones, so that our organisms can (and often do) swing back and forth in response to what is commonly called "stress."

Drugs are agents that affect our nervous system in either one direction or the other. They can be natural hormones like adrenaline, which, if evoked excessively, cause problems such as mood swings and all types of psychosomatic disease, such as headaches, ulcers, heart attacks, and even cancer. Or they may be drugs that we administer from outside our bodies. Either kind can be detrimental. By introducing drugs from outside our body; we may further exacerbate the pendulum-like action in our body chemistry. Heroin depresses the Central Nervous System (CNS) as well as the ANS and our organism compensates down the road by natural body stimulation, which we experience as nervousness. Alcohol works this way too. The stimulant cocaine, used to offset sluggishness, eventually results in more sluggishness and progressively greater cravings for stimulation. This is the vicious cycle of addiction. It can occur by ingesting drugs or by eliciting our own body drugs through habits of excess (in action or even obsessive thinking patterns) that work either as stimulants or depressants. Marijuana, however, doesn't depress the CNS.

The Costa Rican study specifically attempted to find such effects: "One of our principle objectives was to identify gross or subtle changes in major body and Central Nervous System functions... attributable to marijuana. We failed to do so. (W. Carter, edit.)

As an example of the workings of this automatic mechanism: when a threat is perceived, fear is transmitted (via the Hypothalamus) to the body (through the ANS) as an order to prepare for strenuous action. Instantaneously, there is increased Sympathetic energy which pumps adrenaline-like chemicals throughout the entire organism. The heart rate increases dramatically, and the force of the heartbeat becomes greater, to respond to additional needs of the body. More blood with more oxygen is sent immediately to the brain and sense organs (eyes/ears/skin, etc.) for quicker perceptions and decisions. Stored sugars for energy are released by the liver. Capillaries of veins and arteries constrict, especially in the extremities, possibly so that the loss of blood from wounds will be minimized. Blood pressure rises because the veins and arteries have constricted. At the same time the skeletal muscles constrict, almost in an armor-like protective fashion. Breath becomes fast, shallow, noisy and irregular in response to increased energy needs. The pupils of the eyes enlarge for clearer vision. The body has automatically become combat ready without our even knowing it. All we did was get frightened. The ANS did the rest. This body mode is appropriately called the "fight or flight" response (Benson) and is a preparation solely for physical exertion. Once the action is over and the stimulant chemicals have been used, the organism rests at balance. But if no physical response takes place, which often happens in modern life, such as when we react to threats to our own status, ego, profit, etc. (as dangers), the body remains charged by the stimulating chemicals.

The ANS responds in the same way to reality or imagination. Just thinking fearful thoughts enjoins the combat mode through chemical outpourings, and then there is a strong instinctive need to rebalance body chemistry. Our organism is revved up but going nowhere, and we feel tense. The Parasympathetic side of the ANS reduces this tension by an equalizing excessive dose of depressant body chemicals, and then we may feel tired or sluggish. We cannot escape the law of balance. If we become overly excited at first, we become severely depressed later. Such chronic imbalance in the Autonomic System is defined as "stress," experienced physically as contraction or mentally as dissatisfaction, and it is responsible for most modern diseases.

Medicine for the Whole World

So many people, in all walks of life, from all social strata, in every country of the world, from the young to the old (for as long as there has been recorded history) have been and are now partakers of marijuana. They may have considered their enjoyment solely recreational without understanding that this magnificent natural remedy is actually and undeniably (in the strictest sense of the word) a medicine. It is "a substance used to treat disease," where disease is literally loss or lack of "ease" (which defines disruption of the entire person: body/mind/spirit). Marijuana as medicine is especially needed in today's stress-filled, fast-paced, competitive and insecure manner of daily living.

As the way marijuana works (i.e., in complete compatibility with the healthy functioning of all facets of humanness) becomes clear from the scientific presentation on the following pages, it is hoped that the numerous, varied and divided segments of the marijuana population who espouse the employment of Cannabis for different purposes, will realize that medicinal, recreational, and sacramental utilization of this plant are identical. To be healthy is to be happy is to be holy, all of which are connected with Cannabis. Although modern life has divided up the three-fold nature of man and woman, in-fact, there is no division. Our bodies are the temples of the Divine, to be kept in the utmost health, and our minds are the tools by which we recognize the essential values - if we are happy. The path of righteousness and happiness is the Medicine Path!

This book barely addresses the healing that hemp/marijuana could contribute to the deforestation, pollution and devastation of our diseased planet. Not only is Cannabis a superior medicinal remedy for every facet of imbalance in the human organism, it has the potential of serving as a holistic medicine of limitless extensions for healing the earth itself.

Those of us who know the truth have a choiceless commitment to expose it. Our commitment runs as deep as our souls. We enjoin you to further your knowledge and take your place among us.

About The Plant
Of Two Sexes:

The Cannabis Sativa plant evolved during the last part of the Age of the Dinosaurs, over 50 million years ago. By great contrast, the human race is less than 2 million years old (at the very highest estimate).
Cannabis is "dioecious" which means each plant is either a male or a female. Its flowers are called imperfect and incomplete since without a mate, the flower will remain unfinished – without seed. Sinsimilla in its natural environment, Cannabis completes its entire life cycle in one season (annually). No other annual grows faster!

Cannabis Sativa is classified in the flowering plant group of *Angiosperms* which bears its fruit (seed) in a hard, shell-like protective substance. There are between 250,000 and 400,000 flowering plants of all kinds. There are nearly 500 categorizations of "Families" which account for over 99% of the category. Cannabis stands alone in its own family: The Cannabaceae.

Mating: Cannabis Sativa - a Wind-Loving ("anemophilous") Plant
For fertilization to take place, neither the male nor female need ever meet or even be in close proximity. Mating takes place as the male pollen is delivered by the wind to the sticky, thick resin full of cannabinoids that is exuded near the female sex organs. One male Cannabis plant can produce as many as 70,000 pollen grains in each of its hundreds of flowers so that an average-size male plant spews over a billion grains of pollen in any season. Cannabis pollen grains are extremely small and lightweight. Under certain conditions, they can easily travel hundreds of miles - helping Cannabis to be the most adaptable plant in the world in that it grows everywhere and anywhere and adapts to every soil condition and all climates.

Chapter 2 • The Physical Benefits
Marijuana and The Body's
Opposing Modes of Being

The wonder of marijuana is that it works in the body as an antidote to extreme swings. It does not stimulate. It does not depress. It does both at the same time, which is why it is unique, and so misunderstood by a scientific community educated from a narrow dualistic perspective.

The most extensive study of marihuana, written nearly 100 years ago understood the complicated workings of marijuana, when it stated: "It is both sedative and stimulant." (Indian Hemp Drugs Commission)

The simultaneous opposing action of marijuana is akin to balancing our entire system. Such balance in the ANS can be understood as a charged equilibrium, defined as "well-being," experienced as physiological expansion and psychological contentment and responsible for health. (See Charts on pages 30 and 31.)

Many physiological changes occur with marijuana use, yet none of the changes is extreme in any one direction. The action of marijuana in the body causes slower and more expansive breathing (a direct result of Parasympathetic relaxation, which happens to us whenever we become relaxed). At the very same time, the alveoli (sacs in the lungs) expand, so that stale air is better eliminated, allowing for greater oxygen intake (a direct result of more Sympathetic participation, and which happens to us when we become excited), while both slower and deeper breathing occur, the depth of breath is even further aided by relaxing the "oppositional" muscles of the rib cage.

The rationale for health, underlying yogic postures, specifically addresses the benefits attained by increasing the size of the rib cage so as to accommodate an increased oxygen intake. Marijuana relaxes skeletal muscles (including the muscles that constrain the ribs). This efficient breathing has other far-reaching effects. Specifically, the brain receives more richly oxygenated blood and simultaneously receives a greater supply of that blood because of the dilation in all brain capillaries (increased Parasympathetic action). At the same time, because of an increase in Sympathetic energizing the heart rate rises slightly to speed up further the distribution of more richly oxygenated blood. Heart rate increase is usually associated with an increased pulse rate because arteries and veins constrict with Sympathetic activity, but with marijuana no blood pressure rise occurs, since the capillaries have likewise expanded. In essence, the pump exerts a greater force and the enlarged pipes allow for greater flow. The net effect is a highly functioning, yet relaxed, system with better fuel. This is why, with marijuana, the feeling is both relaxed and alert, which explains, in part, the experience of being "stoned."

Normally the body vacillates between the two opposing modes of being. The effects of the complicated marijuana molecule somehow actually integrate these two modes, simultaneously, as absolutely nothing else does, except perhaps Anandamide - which also activates the Cannabinoid Receptors. When we examine the effects of marijuana within the framework of the body's healthy functioning, a dynamic interplay between either excitation or relaxation, we find that both the Relaxation Response and the Fight or Flight mode are enjoined.

The extremes of these two modes are commonly referred to as bipolarity in which one is either depressed or manic. Since Cannabis creates no pendulous action, there is no possibility of it causing physical addiction. It is actually anti-addictive. This explains the mystery of so many regular marijuana users who claim that to stop poses no problem, whatsoever and it confirms all the scientific studies that report no addiction with marijuana.

Marijuana has been successful in treating alcoholics and morphine addicts. "From a limited observation on addicts undergoing morphine withdrawal...the impression was gained that marihuana had beneficial effects." (Mayor La Guardia's Committee) In more recent times, Dr. Tod Mikuriya (under the medical marijuana state law in California) has also reported successfully treating alcoholics with Cannabis. He followed 92 of his patients who were substituting smoked marijuana for alcohol as per his medical recommendation: "It would appear that for selected alcoholics, the substitution of smoked Cannabis for alcohol may be of marked rehabilitative value." The success of his results was dependent on the ease of obtaining marijuana instead of alcohol. If marijuana was not available or too costly, then the addict would turn to alcohol.

Although specific effects of marijuana in the body are well known, each has been taken in isolation without noting that both sides of the Autonomic Nervous System are conjoined. Instead of a perspective that sees the whole person and the simple holistic effect of marijuana, a myopic and reductionistic method of measurement has been employed, and marijuana's profound meaning for health has been lost. Marijuana's action on the balancing mechanism of the human organism is extraordinary, perhaps because of the extreme complexity of the molecule and the uncanny perfect fit with specific receptor sites in the Hypothalamus (Howlett).

It appears that by impacting the ANS at its point of origin, above its locale of bifurcation in the body, marijuana resolves the "relaxation response" and the "fight or flight" reaction into one, thereby producing the subjective experience of unity. The literature concerning the experience of marijuana, from ancient to modern, is full of descriptions of "wholeness" or "oneness" - the paradox of the resolution of opposites.

Opposing Modes of Being
Vacillation between Two Extremes

Sympathetic   Parasympathetic
Overload   Overload

Manic   **Depressed**
Beta Brainwaves   Theta
                                               Brainwaves

"Fight or Flight"   "Lethargic Depression"

Muscles Tight	Muscles Relaxed
Pupils Dilated	Pupils Constricted
Blood Pressure High	Blood Pressure Low
Heart Rate High	Heart Rate Low
Mucus Membranes Dry	Mucus Membranes Wet
Bronchi Dilated	Bronchi Constricted
Veins/Arteries Constricted	Veins/Arteries Dilated
Breathing: Fast, Shallow & Noisy	Breathing: Slow Irregular & Noisy

Patients can be overly excited or depressed.
OUT OF BALANCE

The Marijuana Response
Resolution of the Opposites

SYMPATHETIC – PARASYMPATHETIC BALANCE

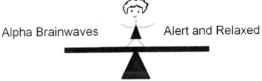

Alpha Brainwaves   Alert and Relaxed

Muscles Relaxed

Pupils Constricted

Blood Pressure Slightly Lowered

Heart Rate Slightly Raised

Mucus Membranes Dry

Bronchi Dilated

Veins/Arteries Dilated

Breathing: Slow, Deep, Regular

WITH MARIJUANA
Patients are relaxed and energized
BALANCE IS RESTORED

Marijuana and the Brain

Just as our Autonomic Nervous System is a two-fold process, so is our brain designed for dual action, with its left hemisphere and right hemisphere. Not surprisingly, these two sides are related to similar differences of action as in the autonomic system. The right side of the brain serves the receptive, creative, and nurturing experiences. We use this side during feelings connected to aesthetics, such as art and music, compassion, and global or spatial reasoning. In the area of cognition, this side adds to our understanding of meaning. The left hemisphere is geared toward linear, analytical, mechanical situations, such as mathematical problems; practical planning; and logical thought. Of course, both sides are always connected in constant communication with each other, and in dynamic complex cooperation. Yet different set and setting cause for greater emphasis in either one side or the other. This is called hemisphericity.

> It is...the idea that a given individual relies more on one mode or hemisphere than on the other. This differential utilization is presumed to be reflected in the individual's cognitive style - the person's preference - approach to problem solving. A tendency to use verbal or analytical approaches to problems is seen as evidence of left-sided hemisphericity, while those who favor holistic or spatial ways of dealing with information are seen as right hemisphere people. (Springer and Deutsch)

Where mechanical activities are constantly fostered, and where attention is geared to competition and acquisition, the workings of the left hemisphere predominate:

> Because we operate iln such a sequential-seeming world and because the logical thought of the left hemisphere is so honored in our culture, we gradually damp out, devalue, and disregard the input of our right hemispheres. It's not that we stop using it altogether; it just becomes less and less available to us because of established patterns. (Prince)

According to Deikman - our most common mode of behavior is "attempting to manipulate the world around us ... through talking, pushing, grasping." He calls this the "hyper-aroused state of mind." The left side of the brain must overwork for most of us, most of the time, while the right brain is under-used, and therefore its special talents are neither appreciated nor cultivated. Studies describe right brain function as:

....silent, dark, intuitive, feeling, spatial, (and) holistic...does not require linear, structured analysis for its knowledge. (And we should note: the right hemisphere is also considered the feminine element, which emphasizes cooperation and non-domination). (Sarawati)

In the materialistic world, such knowledge is basically devalued and denied; except perhaps in the arts. Appropriately, the right hemisphere also includes the creative flashes so often reported by geniuses: "The real thing is intuition. A thought comes and I may try to express it in words afterwards" (Einstein, 1954). But most people perceive an unreality and even irrationality about the intuitive faculty and even feel a great skepticism of it.

Marijuana, by its effect on the ANS, enhances both sides of the brain. Through its increased Sympathetic action, left-brain perception is heightened while, at the same time, right brain reception is enhanced. This is a physiological fact. More blood, and cleaner blood, is sent to the brain as in the "fight or flight" reaction. And because of Parasympathetic dilation of all capillaries, which signifies relaxation, the blood supply of the entire brain is increased. More blood means more oxygen and consequently clearer and broader thinking. Since marijuana works on both sides of the brain, the most noticeable effect, in our fast-paced mindset, is one of slowing down, which blends the thrusting competitive attitude with the contrasting viewpoint of nurturance to arrive at a more cooperative balance. This experience is, however, not innate to marijuana, but to the mental set of the subject. When we are mellow, tired, and relaxed, marijuana is energizing and affords alertness, determination, and even strength. 'This variation in the physiological effects has caused great confusion from an either/or framework. And the balancing nature of marijuana (both/and) has not been understood. It both stimulates and relaxes, simultaneously, which equates to an unpredictable variation in effect that is solely dependent on the state of its subject. When the system is sluggish - as it is for natives in warm climates (Africa, India, South America), marijuana has been used extensively and for centuries to energize it.

A common practice among laborers... (is) have a few puffs at a ganga (marijuana) pipe) to produce well-being, relieve fatigue and stimulate appetite. (Chopra and Chopra)

When the system is hyper-aroused, as in today's lifestyle, marijuana calms. The significance of this fact cannot be ignored. It explains the increased creativity reported as a part of the *marijuana experience*, because when both sides of brain processes are heightened, both types of brain activity are greater. The left-brain notices more, while the right brain receives more. This is the unification of logic and intuition. The term "expansion of consciousness" is explained physiologically as a "shifting of brain emphasis from one-sidedness to balance" (Sugerman and Tarter), which fits precisely with the feeling called "high."

Brain Synchronicity and Marijuana

Stress, as a chronic imbalance in the ANS, shows up as beta waves on an EEG machine and is experienced as worry. Marijuana ingestion has been shown to change the worried state by producing alpha waves, experienced as well being. This is a significant indication of balanced brain functioning because alpha waves occur when at least two waves from different brain loci are rising and falling in phase (in synchrony), as opposed to out-of-phase activity (When waves are non-synchronous). "The EEG begins to report a higher percentage of alpha brain waves as soon as marijuana takes effect." (Ferguson)

The brain waves calm down, and this signifies what scientists have termed "movement from an active to a receptive style" of being (Sugerman and Tarter). This shift correlates with enhancement of all perceptual experiences, because mental clarity proceeds from a relaxed brain wave pattern by allowing thought processes to slow down. As the mind's busyness diminishes, the energy that is usually needed for rapid mental shifts is freed up and becomes available for more intense focusing in attention. A study conducted with marijuana (Halikas) demonstrated that enhancement of sense experience occurs "...as a direct consequence of slower rates of attentional shifts, and an increase of total energy available to consciousness, manifested as intensification of (the contents of) consciousness."

Of course, an evening's marijuana use is not understood with any such analytical recognition. Instead, the felt sensation is of "moreness." In the fast lanes of modern life, where superficial and competitive relationships are all too common, the essence of humanness feels less. Marijuana, by its balancing effect, enriches this dimension of humanness.

Heart, Stomach and Lung Alteration

THE HEART: When we ingest marijuana, the heart swells through capillary enhancement, is fueled more by more fully oxygenated blood, while, at the same time, its contractions and expansions are greater, allowing for stronger pumping action to the rest of the body. In most cultures (ancient and modern), the heart center is designated as the "emotive vortex," which stands for the inner experience and outer expression of human love and affection. Generous and sympathetic people are said to have big hearts. During the *marijuana experience* this is literally the case and allows for the more full-bodied emotions that are in line with the claims of heightened feelings of love and compassion. Once the high is over, the heart is reduced to its usual size. But over a prolonged period, the heart muscle is known to become stronger for having been taxed for short periods. Jogging 20 minutes a day increases the strength of the heart, and to the extent that it is stronger, a jogger's heart displays a slower resting heart beat.

Although no studies have been done on the hearts of marijuana smokers, the odds are that they have stronger hearts too. It would be an easy study to accomplish, if the government would just allow tests to be conducted on a cross section of long-term marijuana users and compare them to the already well-documented statistics of this same age/class disease profile, in this case, the incidence of heart disease. Psychiatric medicine has long realized that tension in the heart area indicates a defensive personality. The suppression of emotions, both tender and angry, is an attempt to ward off pain and puts the individual at risk of heart failure. Marijuana balances this chronic tension by its physiological action on the heart and its calming effects on the entire body.

THE STOMACH AND LUNGS: A tense stomach is the physical counterpart of mental tension and results in digestive problems (ulcers, colitis, stomach cancer, obesity, constipation, etc.). The mental tension is displayed through obsessing (or ruminating) over threats to one's welfare, resulting in excessive and continuous digestive messages (excessive Parasympathetic). Just as a cow chews its cud, or ruminates (always digesting in one of its four stomachs), so one who worries "eats" away at his or her innards. Psychologically, this implies an inability to let go of fear for oneself. Physiologically, the insecurity can be observed in the pattern and depth of the breath: "Shallow breathing can act as a personal defense against the experience of feeling" (Dychtwald)

Shallow breathing is noticed at the level of the stomach, because the diaphragm is the muscle of breath. If one does not breathe with the movement of the diaphragm, suppression of the breath takes place. Likewise, the stomach is stagnant. Over time, with continued "holding" or breathing contraction, the stomach loses its motility. This occurs as a response to feared situations and to a greater or lesser degree becomes chronic in early years, in all populations where perfect balance is not encouraged:

> Very young children breathe with little inhibition or disturbance of natural breathing rhythms. But as one grows up, he/she experiences traumas, imitates others, follows erroneous advice, and thereby develops incorrect breathing habits. These lead to chronic distortions in the breathing pattern and consequently to disequilibrium in other functions. Most adults breathe irregularly or they chronically tense some of the muscles involved in the breathing process. (Aiaya)

According to Rosenberg and Rand:

> Breathing deeply and fully amplifies awareness of feelings. Many of the feelings that emerge with the deep breathing are uncomfortable, so most people avoid awareness by restricting their breathing.

When the ANS becomes habituated to Imbalance, as a direct result of chronic breathing distortion, the problem usually results from restricted exhalation. An organism that does not empty itself cannot refill. The term "anal-retentive" describes the syndrome of being unable to "let go," or relax, as a habitual attitude toward life. Because of the complex interactions that occur throughout the body, once the breath is disturbed, various dysfunctions follow. In the digestive system, restriction of peristalsis results both from a subdued breath and skeletal muscular tension. Restriction in the exchange of carbon dioxide and oxygen, which is what happens with a shallow breath pattern, likewise adds to digestive disease, as ANS functioning is skewed toward sympathetic imbalance. The net result is nervousness (sympathetic overload) or depression (parasympathetic overload). Stomach problems correspond to ANS imbalance at either extreme. With excessive stimulants as with an over-abundance of sympathetic chemicals, breathing imbalance results in diminished messages sent to the digestive system. Whereas with Parasympathetic overload, breathing imbalance results in excessive messages to the digestive system; either one of these surpluses eventually results in excessiveness at the other extreme. Marijuana is an agent that can mitigate these extreme swings in the ANS. And therein is the reason that marijuana, not so long ago, was commonly prescribed for all sorts of digestive disturbances.

Patterns of shallow breathing have been studied to show that the less the body is supplied with superior oxygen, the less it is able to cope with threatening situations, physical or mental (Canon). Such shallow breathing is affected by chronically not breathing out sufficiently and is a direct result of restricted diaphragmatic movement. Inhalation, on the other hand, is secondary to exhalation, so that we breathe in, in direct correlation to the capacity exhaled. With asthma patients, who have trouble exhaling, marijuana facilitates exhalation:

> The fact that marijuana increases the diameter of bronchi in a manner unlike that of standard anti-asthmatic agents makes its further Investigation desirable. (Health and Human Services)

Once the toxins in the lungs are more efficiently released, obtaining sufficient oxygen by deep and full breathing follows automatically. As rigidity in the body is released or reduced by the action of marijuana, there is a corresponding reduction of mental tension that translates into a feeling of expansion and well-being and explains the reverential attitude commonly expressed by marijuana lovers.

Medico-Pharmaceutical Interpretation of Recent Studies:
Marijuana reduces the plaque in arteries – Explanation of the scientists lean toward the anti-inflammatory properties of THC. Also – **Synthetic cannabinoid causes neurogenesis** (growth of neurons in the brain) and reduces anxiety and depression. In addition, studies show**: Brain tumors – eliminated with Cannabis** in one third of test rats. (This cancer kills patients in a year since no effective treatment exists.) Cannabis stimulates the immune system to attack the cancerous cells, according to the scientists. **HOWEVER:**
Researchers: "Cannabis should not be considered a treatment option" (since they are not certain how it works).
 "To extrapolate this to, "A joint a day will keep the doctor away,' I think is premature," (Dr Libby, Boston's Women's Hospital). "When one smokes (Cannabis) only a small part of the cannabinoids are expected to reach the tumor." And "These results may provide the basis for a new therapeutic approach for the treatment of malignant gliomas." (Manuel Guzman)

The Plant

The Seed
Fertilization from the pollen grain occurs within 15 to 20 minutes of mating, and may take up to two days in cool temperatures. As soon as conception is assured, the cells begin to coalesce around the embryo to create the hard coating around the seed and to supply it with the needed nutrients for developing. A mature female Cannabis Sativa plant can produce tens of thousands of seeds!

Nothing in the vegetable world contains the incredible balanced nutrition of the Cannabis Seed. It has a full spectrum of "essential fatty acids" and all the amino acids necessary for animal life. Its unique nutrient and vitamin abundance is ripened in the sun yet shielded from predators by the thick cannabinoid-concentrated resin. Research indicates that Cannabis can withstand the UV Rays of the sun specifically because of the constant oozing shield of its unique secretions; and that the oily strong-smelling compounds probably serve to ward off dehydration, disease and nutritional loss.

This is hardly a plant more adjustable than Cannabis. As climate, diseases, and pests change, the stain evolves and selects new defenses, programmed into the genetic orders contained in each generation of seeds.

Chapter 3 • Psychological Benefits
Perceiving: Sense Organs

As the body's workings can become more harmonious with marijuana, the functioning of the five senses can be noticeably improved. This naturally occurs, as the organs of sense are fueled with more oxygenated blood, as well as being less constrained or constricted. The eyes, the ears, the skin, the nose, and the taste buds are supplied with more and better "fuel" during the *marijuana experience*. There is nothing mysterious or mystical about the subjective feelings that all marijuana users report, such as: finer appreciation of visual and auditory stimuli (art and music); more enhanced sense of taste and appetite; greater feelings of tenderness and eroticism (sex is better); and a deeper and more insightful understanding of all experience, including our own thoughts and emotions.

> Appetite is regulated by the hypothalamus, where marijuana works directly. This is parasympathetic energizing, which aids sugar storage (i.e., it takes it out of our blood stream and saves it in the liver) and is therefore responsible for appetite increase. Owing to a greater supply of oxygenated blood to taste buds (Parasympathetic energizing), there is greater appreciation and enjoyment of food. Stimulants (such as cocaine) release our body's supply of stored sugars (which depletes us) into the blood stream and kill our appetite. Of course, the taste buds constrict with all body excitement, and therefore food is less enjoyable.

> Grass (marijuana) ... heightens your enjoyment of your perceptions and conceptions... (it) causes the feeling of just being alive...There are four areas in which this heightening of the sexual response is clearly manifest; foreplay, control, orgasm and creativity. (Margolis and Clorfene)

This enhanced capacity of all the body's sense organs (including the sense one has of him/herself) accounts for the mental interpretation of intense perceptions, known as the "high." Technically speaking" this is really a (marvelous) side effect to balancing the ANS. In our discussion, the trigger to the high experience is marijuana, but many other activities also can also produce it, such as jogging, chanting, fasting, isolation, meditation, and prayer. Life's precious moments represent entry to the "high," such as the birth of a child, the rediscovery of romance, and even witnessing a beautiful sunset.

> Altered states of consciousness can be triggered by hypnosis, psychedelics, deep prayer, sensory deprivation, acute psychosis; sleep deprivation, fasting, epileptic attacks and migraines, hypnotic monotony, electronic brain stimulation, alpha training, clairvoyance, muscle relaxation, isolation, photic stimulation and kundalini yoga. (Ferguson)

Another component to the intensification of sensory perceptions and mental understanding can be understood by the equilibrium marijuana produces in brain functioning. The *marijuana experience* is innately connected to the mental set and environmental setting of the subject. As we have seen, marijuana works toward equalizing ANS energizing, which in our fast-paced world will be toward receptivity and away from the striving, grasping, hurried and active mode of being. When this takes place, our rate of attentional shifting also slows down. The energy that it takes to maintain the active, aggressive mode is therefore likewise freed up:

> One of the most commonly reported effects of marijuana is the enhancement of perceptual experiences - auditory, gustatory, tactual, olfactory...visual experiences are reported as occurring in a more intense fashion.
>
> These phenomena are expected as a direct consequence of slower rate of attentional shifts, and they may be supported by an increase in total energy...if not used to produce attentional shifts, is available to consciousness. (Halikas, Goodwin and Guze)

The great sense of insight produced by marijuana is also explained by Sugerman and Tarter as resulting from a slower rate of shifting one's attention, thereby in the act of "thinking," the thoughts "will be imbued with enhanced intensity."

Another faculty, sometimes called the sixth sense, is our undeveloped capacity for perceiving the world and its meaning. This is the dimension of intuition, or deeper-than-usual understanding with which poets and saints are familiar. The marijuana user becomes aware of this sense. Many artistic and creative people claim this as the single most beneficial aspect of using marijuana.

> Although most scientific authors who present new respectable evidence for the harmlessness of marihuana use make no claim for its surprising usefulness. I do make that claim: Marihuana is a catalyst for specific optical and aural aesthetic perceptions. I appreciate the structure of certain pieces of jazz and classical music in a new manner under the Influence of marihuana, and these apprehensions have remained valid in years of normal consciousness. (Ginsberg)

Development of the sixth sense merges with, harkens, and even hastens, spiritual development and may easily lead to reverence for the plant that brings this radiance:

The Report of the Indian Hemp Drugs' Commission, conducted by the Indian and Great British Governments was the most extensive examination of marijuana to date - some of the significant statements from that massive work, which represented the entire Indian cultural orientation over the course of its 5000-year-intact civilization concerning the reverent attitude toward marijuana include:

> To the Hindu, the hemp plant is holy...a guardian lives in the marihuana leaf...its thought bracing qualities show...(it) is the home of the great Yogi ...its powers give (ganja) a high place among lucky objects... Oaths are taken on its leaf...spirit of bhang (marihuana) is the spirit of freedom and knowledge...(is) the cleanser of ignorance ...students of the scriptures at Benares are given bhang ([marijuana and milk beverage) before they sit to study...(to) center their thoughts on the Eternal. (Indian Hemp Drugs' Commission)

Mental Balance

The novice cannot fully appreciate the *marijuana experience*, since it takes time to realize the association between heightened capacities and Cannabis. Yet the mental states that occur with *pot* are neither unfamiliar nor mysterious. Although, Anandamide, the naturally occurring brain hormone, was only recently discovered, its effects have always been part of the human experience. These effects are subtle and for that reason scientists have not even known to search for them. Only because of the THC encoding of the cannabinoid receptor in the brain did it become clear that the brain, itself, must have its own key. That is why none of the changes of marijuana taken separately are different from what we experience every day.

> It is striking that so many...medical reports failed to mention any intoxicating properties of (marijuana). Rarely, if ever, is there any indication that patients - hundreds of thousands of them who received Cannabis in Europe in the nineteenth century - were "stoned" or changed their altitudes toward work, love, their fellow man, or their homelands. (Tart)

Instead, it is the totality of the subtle changes that are notable and noticed, but noticed only after one focuses attention:

> Typically the first few times a person smokes marijuana...the overall pattern of his consciousness stays quite ordinary and he (or she) usually wonders why others make so much fuss. Natural feelings of expansion that correspond to favorable perceptions, such as a sense of accomplishment, are experiences common to us all. What makes marijuana unique and beneficial is its ability to summon these states of well being at will. Anandamide may well be blocked from being secreted effectively or received appropriately once the organism has become habituated to disequilibrium. By re-summoning the lost ability to gain balance through the *marijuana experience*, the bliss of life may be reawakened. From such a positive point of view, problems are understood and more easily resolved when tranquility is coupled with insight. The regular marijuana user reaches these states of tranquility over and over again, leading to a fuller integration of the person with his/her environment.

According to Maslow, who developed a theoretical framework to measure high-functioning adults, or as he termed them "self-actualizers," certain, few members of a society reach a more mature or "more fully human" state as a way of life. His paradigm presents a hierarchy of goals for the developing individual, with "basic human needs" as only the first stage to be mastered along an ascension that culminates in "meta motives" or goals of a higher, more artistic, less self-centered, more individualistic nature. Self-actualizers are those who have gratified basic needs and are, therefore, no longer motivated by them. Instead higher motivations are their goals. Self-actualizers represent a small percentage of society who exhibit greater degrees of health and joy than is common for most people. However, virtually everyone has had an exalted, expanded period of consciousness triggered by "music/beauty/luck." These times of happiness and well-being he terms "peak experiences" and notes that they are usually forgotten, since no importance is attached to them. We might suggest that those hundreds of millions of people around the world who use marijuana to experience higher levels of life, do so specifically because of the great import they ascribe to being "high", i.e., feeling better, happier, more expansive, and therefore, more tolerant and compassionate.

Although we commonly refer to the body, mind, and spirit as separate entities, these divisions do not really exist. The roots, branches, and leaves serve the same purpose when we are discussing different facets of *tree-ness*. But to appreciate the concept of tree, the entire entity must be considered. No one would ever logically argue that the leaves exist separate from branches or roots, or that the health of the leaves is not innately connected to the health of the roots. Holistic health is a return to a basic age-old notion of wholeness that existed throughout history. It views a person in the same fashion that a botanist sees a tree. It is "all of a piece," and any division that is allowed is done so for the sole purpose of simplifying discussion. We can see, then, that as the body's modus operandi is altered during the *marijuana experience*, the mind's processes likewise change.

Psychological Marijuana Experience

Accepting that psychological defense mechanisms correspond to body tension, obviously it doesn't matter in what sphere the alteration begins, since they are two sides of the same coin and therefore affect each other completely. According to Elmer Green:

> Every change in the physiological state is accompanied by an appropriate change in the mental-emotional state, conscious or unconscious... and conversely, every change in the mental-emotional state, conscious or unconscious is accompanied by an appropriate change in the physiological state. (Ferguson)

When the body relaxes, so does the mind. But releasing tension and inhibitions via drunkenness and/or tranquilization is accompanied by numbing normal consciousness, leading to a state of unawareness. Whereas marijuana results in an "altered state of consciousness," the depressant drugs have been described as producing "altered states of unconsciousness" (Sugerman and Tarter) allowing for relaxation without awareness.

As a consequence of the capacity of individual thought, each of us maintains a personal unconsciousness, which comprises repressed issues that often contradict the image we have of ourselves. The unconscious mind can be exposed in dreams or by drinking alcohol to excess. It can reveal itself in psychoanalysis, meditation, and during the consciousness fostered by marijuana, as well as in times of extreme stress (as in nervous breakdown), and during life-threatening experiences. The unconscious is exposed by breaking down the barrier between it and the conscious mind. This barrier is commonly called "defense mechanisms" or "armor" by Western psychology, so named by the famed psychologist Wilhelm Reich.

The healthiest person is depicted as one who has very few defense mechanisms that shield him/her from unsavory aspects of the hidden personality. It follows that the healthy person will not need to invest much energy in keeping out unconscious motives/fears/memories from conscious awareness and will be therefore more broad-minded, or as they say, "less defended." In the field of psychology, optimum health implies total vulnerability to all facets of personality, where the unconscious blends with the conscious to form an "integrated" person. Carl Jung explained it as a blending of the "persona" (outward personality) with the "shadow" (or internal side of human nature), so that nothing of the self remained in the dark - hidden from awareness.

Marijuana exposes things. When used over a period of time, it allows us to witness our many subtle motives, which, under normal consciousness, are usually not noticeable. The *marijuana experience* seems to open the curtain to our self-deceptions, and gives us access to our innermost private agendas. "Alcohol primarily relieves anxiety and promotes optimism. It makes the society and what one has to do with society OK. Pot, on the other hand, turns you inside yourself" (Freidenberg).

The traditional Western modality of treating neurosis has a director or outer authority as the witness (in the form of the therapist), Neurosis is understood as the dark, dangerous side of ourselves that conflicts with our attitudes and ideals, but with which everyone must somehow come to terms, if he/she is to become whole. Rejection of the dark side is the neurotic "division in personality, and hostility between conscious or unconscious." (Rosenberg) In the more liberal Transpersonal Psychology (adapted from Eastern Theory), the "patient" is a student and attends to his/her own conflicts, as in meditation or yoga. Self-responsibility is the main difference between the two schools of psychology. In yoga psychology one needs to learn on one's own, rather than be shown by an authoritarian figure - who represents the fuel for change. Meditation is the ultimate tool for self-knowledge. In the East, marijuana has been used to facilitate the process for millennia:

> Cannabis plays a very significant role in the meditative ritual used to facilitate deep meditation and heighten awareness...use of hemp is likewise so common now (1979) in this region (Tibet) that the plant is taken for granted as an everyday necessity. (Schultes and Hofmann)

It was just this catalytic effect of marijuana - to expose the unconscious and increase the patient's vulnerability, while maintaining awareness and understanding – that prompted psychologists (in the 60s and 70s) to utilize marijuana extensively in their therapeutic studies before the government ban. Understanding one's motives over time, and with active registration, serves to encourage the ability to look past usual defensive positions.

Optimum psychological health ("ego strength") is evidenced by full integration of the unconscious within the realm of awareness: "The problem is simply to open the channels between the conscious and unconscious minds" (Weil). It can also be realized as accepting or loving (all of) oneself totally without judgment.

Anything that enhances the functioning of the body also mitigates mental tension; with a "witnessing" aspect, there exists the possibility of learning and growth within the personality. Loosening of defense mechanisms automatically changes the notion of the self (I-ness) since awareness expands to include repressed fears and forgotten needs. At times, the experience of seeing ourselves in an unfavorable light can be painful. At other times, when we are not focused on our shortcomings, a less defended viewpoint frees up the energy that maintained the repression. The experience of the NOW is intensified with marijuana, because of the increased psychic energy available to perceive the moment. This intensification is the summation of all the effects that have accrued to the entire body-mind. When it (the high) occurs with marijuana, much of its emphasis is due to the immediacy of the change. Enhanced sense perception (including the mental sense of oneself) occurs as soon as the marijuana takes effect (in minutes when smoked and an hour if ingested). It is like suddenly operating without resistance (i.e., without muscle-armor or mental-tension) and implies a gentler outlook than is usual. This explains why marijuana is associated with peace rather than aggression and probably explains the worry of detractors who claim a loss of the competitive spirit with Cannabis use:

> Marijuana is symbolic of a more passive, contemplative and less competitive attitude toward life than has been traditional in the U.S. It is usually denounced by people who like things the way they are. (Snyder)

The balanced personality (of "extreme health") has not been studied by traditional psychology, which up to now has focused on the conflicts of neurotic populations. In the 1960s and 70s, with the emergence of the Humanistic psychologies, formal theory developed to include health as a natural progression in human growth (See Maslow, May, Tart, Ornstein).

Holistic health (with its emphasis on wellness rather than sickness) is an outgrowth of this orientation. Its goal is balance, as contrasted with suppressing the symptoms of illness (imbalance). The methods are varied, but always include self-regulation and responsibility on the part of the student, reduction of tension through healthy relaxation methods, and replacement of dysfunctional breathing patterns.

> We have been able to confirm repeatedly Wilhelm Reich's observation that psychological resistance and defenses use the mechanism of restricting the breathing. Respiration has a special function among the physiological functions of the body. It is an autonomous function, but it can easily be influenced after volition, increase of the rate and the depth of breathing typically loosens the psychological defenses and leads to release and emergence of the unconscious (and super conscious) material. (Grof)

Less tense populations tend toward greater appreciation of the moment, are less apt to accept a hurried way of life, and more prone to creative pursuits. This accounts for the widespread use of marijuana among artists, musicians, and populations less interested in power and more interested in self-expression and human relationship. It also probably explains why very competitive and rigid people are so against the *marijuana experience*, since these personality types are innately anxious and suspicious of change. Imbalance becomes fixed, familiar, and even comfortable, whereas balance is feared as the unknown. According to Melamede, the extreme intolerance toward all forms of fuller expression can be traced to an operational deficit in the Cannabinoid System.

With marijuana, balance is especially startling, because it occurs quickly and effortlessly. This effect alone is most likely responsible for the fear of the "work ethic" against marijuana. To arrive at the feeling of well-being without hard work or pain seems immoral in the West. This arises from the foolish notion that happiness (or wellness) is unnatural, even sinful, and is based on accentuated alienation from the "whole" of life. On the other hand, a holistic orientation envisions higher states of happiness as the natural birthright of human beings.

Marijuana Benefits are Long Term

The benefits of marijuana are far ranging, long term, and not as instantaneous as the "high." In the short run the equilibrium that occurs is only temporary and reverses as soon as the "high" wears off.

Conscious realization of one's hidden motives and defenses is not effortless, but includes emotional pain. The *marijuana experience* itself does not miraculously cure. Instead it allows the body a respite from the tensions of imbalance, while exposing the mental confusion of the mind. Although, in the short run, balance is easily lost, the essential tendency to homeostatic habituation (health) develops over time. In the long run, then, marijuana can serve as the vehicle by which the body-mind heals itself. This is not to suggest that all one needs to do is smoke pot to dissolve the illness of years. What takes place, instead, is subtle and long term. With the expansiveness that occurs with marijuana, the subject may begin to notice infinite possibilities to raise the quality of his/her life that would otherwise have remained hidden from normal, defensive consciousness. And feelings of health and happiness naturally lead to hope, which of itself can be curative.

The *marijuana experience* of balance becomes a learned and, over time, somewhat permanent, response as the essential human tendency to homeostasis is reawakened and the natural healing process restored. A person who breathes, thinks, and feels healthier for a short time, with no adverse consequence (discounting the discomfort that may accompany fuller awareness), is certainly better off for the experience. And if persons habitually breathe, think, and feel healthier, through meditation, marijuana, vegetarianism or what have you, they begin to face toward health, whether or not they continue any particular practice. In other words, it is better to have used marijuana and stopped, than never to have used it at all. But of course, it is best to use marijuana regularly:

> Any process or method that helps defuse the toxicity of a stressful event or situation is good. (Wallace)

Mental Imbalance

A deep sense of insecurity exists in most lives. The sadness of death perhaps never completely loses its influence over us. We develop all kinds of conscious and unconscious anxieties associated · with that aversion. Often times, these influence us, buried as they are like a basement furnace that keeps everything warm without a visible flame. Awareness of such fears is discouraged, for it causes pain. Defenses keep these insecurities hidden beneath a facade of competence and/or confidence, creating the neurotic personality. The amount off fear, and how successfully it is repressed, determines the vulnerability of a particular subject to a state of "paranoia." The more we have a deluded sense of self-esteem, the greater the possibility for panic. Another way of understanding paranoid reactions is from an energetic model. As the conscious mind habitually represses unconscious motives, energy to do so can be likened to a dam that holds back the floodwater. The slightest break in the dam signals a lessening of the holding strength, which consequently loosens the floodgates. Marijuana can act as the loosening agent, so that whatever has been banned from consciousness may come cascading forth. To uncover our deceptions without our usual rationalizations can be unpleasant, an experience that has turned many psychologically fragile individuals away from marijuana despite its therapeutic catharsis.

Predictably, if we continue to unleash that which is repressed, deep-seated fears can be worked out and resolved. Just as when a dam is dismantled, the floodwater no longer holds power but is instead merged in the larger river, so too does insecurity lose its strength to manipulate us unawares, when it is incorporated into conscious recognition. With awareness, conflict can be dealt with, allowing us greater freedom in action.

Almost everyone has learned what life's expectations are by the time they are three or four years old. Already by that age a certain "cluster of tendencies" - certain desires or feelings have been subdued in order to attain/maintain approval and love. The more we need love (or feel unloved), the more we strive toward the ideal image that we have internalized in our earliest years. Accepting and adopting standards of behavior is the process of "civilizing" that all healthy and energetic children resist, in one way or another. As development progresses, this "cluster of hidden tendencies" assumes a life of its own. It becomes the shadow of the front presented to the world. The front is Jung's "persona" that the outside world can see. What is invisible is the shadow: all that has been chronically denied as we ascend the ladder to neurotic maturity and adulthood.

Regardless of the model used, marijuana resolves conflict by de-emphasizing extreme aggressiveness and stroking the receptive sides of human nature. This unification or balance, however, may be responsible for changes in goals and values. It is the healthy balancing nature of marijuana that is most beneficial to the individual and most threatening to modern society. According to Bromberg:

(The Protestant ethic)...in this country condemns marijuana as an opiate used solely for pleasure (whereas) alcohol is accepted because it lubricates the wheels of commerce and catalyzes social intercourse... marijuana's effect in producing a state of introspection and bodily passivity is repellant to a cultural tradition that prizes activity, aggressiveness, and achievement. (Mayor LaGuardia's Committee)

Social Imbalance

Our entire society may be viewed as one of denial, fearful of unspoken and unresolved issues. The fear of drug use, without an understanding of its basic cause, its function, and its deeply felt need explains today's mindset. If we examine the Systems Theory in psychology, this can be more clearly understood. Any system, be it a family, an office group, or a society may operate in dysfunction. As a repressed family is sick and naturally influences its children in the direction of its imbalance, so does a civilization that is operating from disequilibrium produce a citizenry that is sick. "The addiction (imbalance) is catching" (Schaef).

We need just to look at the unwholesome food/programs/drugs that are our daily bread, to realize the universality of the cultural imbalance. We learn to breathe, think, and eat within the structure of our life situation. Our modern culture has been similarly called materialistic, denying, or competitive. Our citizens die of cancer, heart attacks, and hypertension, all of which can be classified as diseases of disequilibrium, directly compatible with sympathetic overload, expressed as competition, and called *stress*. The overlay of today's values is skewed in the direction of acquisition, born of an attitude of fear and protectiveness. Our children are immediately taught that being smart is eminently more important than being fair. To be "number one," i.e., to gain financial success by overpowering other people's productivity, vision, and determination, is the American Dream. Intrinsic human values are given lip service, but nowhere in our educational system are children taught to look inward so as to develop a core of principles and a systematic method to realize them. Instead, we bombard our children's intellects with ever-faster computer games, programs for the gifted, continuous TV, video-games and constant activities, all of which aid acceleration of linear thought. To accommodate to this mode of living, everyone is necessarily "geared up," or stimulated. Anything that slows down the process is devalued or denied. Although marijuana can help to rebalance the personality, through direct, measurable benefits to the psychological/physical organism, such an effect threatens the social agenda. The citizens who cannot cope become the sacrifice. They are often the hardest working, fastest living, stoic types who develop cancer or die suddenly from heart failure. Their mechanical orientation cannot be changed by whim or will. They are who they are, and they represent the very striving by which the society fuels itself. To maintain the culture's status quo, health and happiness must be compromised. Ironically, marijuana, so beneficial to balance of the body and peace of the mind, endangers the very core of capitalism. "Drugs of unconsciousness," and especially alcohol, which anesthetize the psychological pain, and block out the causes of a repressive society, are much more acceptable. The fact that in the long run they destroy many lives needs to be overlooked because they don't interfere with the overall values of society and are relied upon by many "respectable" addicts to relieve their internal stress, especially severe in industrialized societies.

The social paranoia that marijuana has met with is surely under-standable. To a society skewed toward constant pressure, the idea of slowing down is frightening. The observation has often been made that the use of marijuana "kills ambition," "makes us sleepy," and generally makes us less concerned with worldly goings-on. "It slows me down" is the often-heard complaint, or just as often. "I get sleepy;" A comparison to the Western viewpoint on pain is appropriate. Take a pill – never mind searching out the source of the problem. Subdue the symptom -ignore the cause - and even deny the foolhardiness of such a philosophy. Marijuana is an agent that balances the Autonomic Nervous System. Is it possible that the "slowing down" and the nap are the organisms turning toward health? A relaxed attitude is only harmful to the goals of a workaholic. Excessive competition feeds stress and cannot be the healthiest and happiest way to live. Then the argument turns to: "If everyone smoked pot, would the whole world stop functioning?" The world would certainty not fall apart, even if, by some miracle, everyone did smoke pot. Imagine the possibilities for cooperation throughout the world that might occur, if everyone somehow had a slightly higher consciousness that included "you as well as me." Of course, from an acquisitive position, this would be quite unprofitable. Nevertheless, the higher values of non-aggression are always present somewhere in the human psyche, as difficult as they may be to retrieve. Study upon study has shown that less violence is associated with marijuana use than any legal substance used for recreation.

Marijuana is much less likely than alcohol to produce aggressive behavior. Neither the marijuana user nor the drug itself can be said to constitute a danger to public safety. For, whatever an individual is, in all of his (and her) cultural, social and psychological complexity is not going to vanish in a puff of marijuana smoke. (Mayor LaGuardia's Committee)

Just as significantly, in exact opposition to the excessive maligning of marijuana, all studies support the fact that nothing important is ever forgotten or neglected because of the use of marijuana. People can drive, take care of their children, write legal briefs and perform meaningfully at their jobs, and just as brilliantly at their studies, if they are regular marijuana users. Marijuana does not debilitate one's behavior, as alcohol/tranquilizers/speed/cocaine do. From the Secretary of Health and Human Services:

In the politicized and emotionally charged atmosphere surrounding Marijuana use, far too much research has been marred by the predetermined stance of the researchers. Much that claims to be research is barely above polemics. Fully aware of this problem, we tried to look as objectively as possible at the consequences of long term heavy use. We employed natural, as well as clinical settings, used an unprecedented number of carefully matched subjects. Our measures were as thoughtfully chosen as we could make them. None of us who directed the project had any preconceived notions as to what we might find. We were entering a new field of research and were willing and anxious to accept any data or insights that might emerge.

Many of us were frankly surprised that we were unable to uncover any real consequences of prolonged use.... Indeed, some... were sincerely disappointed at the lack of significant differences between our controlled population of uses and nonusers.

But no findings in science are in themselves findings, indeed findings of the most important type. For years, those of us who made up the research team had assimilated the pseudo-scientific reports of the popular press to the effects that marijuana use, over time, could lead to a frightening array of deleterious effects. We had frankly expected to find at least some of these in our research. Yet the fact that we did not is entirely in keeping with results of the only other serious studies of chronic effects in which intervening socio-cultural variables have been properly controlled, namely, those studies carried out in Greece and Jamaica. Had we looked at almost any other substance, alcohol, for instance, we would have found more effects that we found with marijuana... Overall the findings indicated that the level of marijuana has little influence on performance in neuropsychological intelligence, and personality battery. (Carter)

The Mayor's Committee also confirmed lack of deleterious effects:

The publicity concerning...catastrophic effects of marijuana smoking in New York City is unfounded...the marijuana users accustomed to daily smoking for a period of from two and a half to sixteen years, showed no abnormal system functioning which would differentiate them from non-users. There is definite evidence in this study that the marijuana users were not inferior in intelligence to the general population and that they had suffered no mental or physical deterioration as a result of their use of the drug... The use of marijuana does not lead to morphine or heroin or cocaine addiction and no effort is made to create a market for these narcotics by stimulating the practice of marihuana smoking.

According to Sugerman & Tarter:

Should memory be sampled under the influence of marijuana, it could be done with greater intensity... with a greater flow and with deeper-lying or unusual associations brought to consciousness. Nevertheless, virtually all studies completed to date show no evidence at all of chronically impaired neuropsychological test performance in humans at dose level experimentally studied... In a study of chronic Greek users, a different technique was employed to determine whether brain atrophy might be present in heavy users. The findings were negative: that is, users were not found to differ from non-users in evidence of gross brain pathology.

The truth is the majority of people do not use marijuana to revolutionize their way of life. Instead, they enjoy its physiological relaxant effect unawares, and appreciate the sense of mental well being that accompanies the experience. Depending upon the variety of marijuana that is employed - Sativa or Indica - this sense of well-being has subtle variations; especially in Homeopathic medical treatment, in the 19th century and early 20th century, differences between the two strains were recognized.

When it first became popular in the West, marijuana was imported mainly from tropical zones, where the Sativa strain of Cannabis is indigenous. This type of marijuana is known for its "cerebral high," having little noticeable body participation. Recently, studies have shown that the differences between the two types of Cannabis are relevant in treating specific maladies. With the Sativa strain, it is reasonable to assume more sympathetic or stimulant qualities than Indica (a cooler climate type). This is compatible with the notion than in hotter climates; less calming is desirable from a recreational substance, since hot climates in themselves cause lethargy. Many connoisseurs of marijuana prefer the Sativa high, although in the last decade it has become very scarce due to domestic cultivation of strains that thrive in temperate zones. "Cerebral highs" are experienced as lightness of thought beyond usual concern with self-esteem. In relationships, a cerebral high attunes the participants to a less separate sense of others. Conversation is animated and a general feeling of camaraderie is in the air.

The Indica strain of Cannabis offers more of the "body high." Depth rather than height best describes the subjective experience. Rather than freedom in the mind, the felt sensation is freedom of the body. This state more closely mimics deep relaxation. Thought patterns do not approach the clarity of thought of a "cerebral high." In contrast, the "body high" is similar to the reverie that precedes sleep. While thinking may be diminished, more sensitivity to nonverbal experiences, such as music and color, comes into play. Physiologically, a true "body high" probably is the result of more parasympathetic input. Participants often become quieter, since internal silence predominates.

Indica thrives in temperate areas, and as such it has become more popular with the American marijuana farmer. It is a shorter variety, thus it is more suited for the limits of indoor gardens and comes to fruition earlier in outdoor gardens. In less tropical zones, recreational substances are compatible with tempering the bustle usual to cooler climate cultures. As horticultural interest has grown, a cross between the Indica and Sativa "species" of Cannabis has given the modern marijuana user the subtleties of both strains. Nowadays quality marijuana, grown in the U.S., is usually a hybrid of Indica and Sativa varieties.

Marijuana and Mental Processes

Marijuana will not tolerate repression. Tranquilizers and depressants· relax the body and release tension, but the state of mind associated with these drugs is "unconsciousness" whereby we escape rather than resolve our dilemmas. Alcoholism is an extreme need of both the body and personality periodically to release the nervousness that has accumulated and continues to accumulate to an unbearable degree. It serves the same function for the collective personality of the society, as well. A culture in which alcohol and tranquilizers are the prevalent form of release prefers not to witness internal confusion and actually chooses to act without conscious participation, maintaining a semi-numb condition. One feels less pressure, expresses less emotion and is less able to care – all as a consequence of being less conscious. This type of relaxation releases conflict without knowledge of its source, treating the symptom while ignoring the cause. The uncovering of inner confusion, so prominent with marijuana, is conspicuously absent with depressants. As the overall benefits of insightfulness obtained from its use lead to a greater freedom, marijuana is shunned by individuals who need the status quo in the personality or social position.

Sigmund Freud developed and expounded the understanding that we mechanically base our actions on programs devised throughout life, and many esoteric schools, ancient and modern, have taught the same. Being aware of these programs is very difficult, since ordinary consciousness has within it the conspiracy to keep the mind comfortable and free of conflict. This operates collectively, as well as individually. Whenever confronted, this usual state of mind automatically assumes a defensive posture by relying on distorted rationalizations, which are evident in a repressive and intolerant social order. By contrast, the open and aware consciousness often leads to spiritual realizations, irrelevant in mainstream thinking. In today's world this understanding is uncommon. Higher morals and ethics, as propounded by organized religions, are agreed upon by the masses, especially during church attendance, but are otherwise too difficult to maintain when personal survival is at stake. Universal spiritual values, so often released with marijuana, can break down the conditioned defensive mentality.

It appears as if society, as well as the programmed, individual mind, needs to hold in check the notion that we love our neighbor as ourselves. There is no way that we can love our neighbor as ourselves, nor any way that our economy can subscribe to a policy of cooperation, when the very life of business enterprise is dependent upon "profit first and foremost." Cooperation within free enterprise is a difficult reality so long as "me first" remains the primary motivation. A neurotic society, with its deeply imbedded habit of maladaptive coping methods, is resistant to change. Marijuana can be of tremendous benefit in exposing the distorted perspectives responsible for social, class, and racial conflict. It can open the "doors of perception," and thereby alter the very core of the personality, by allowing a view of the transcendent values of human life.

Cannabis is anathema to the dominant culture because it de-conditions or decouples users from accepted values. When pursued as a lifestyle (it) places a person in intuitive contact with less goal oriented and less competitive behavior patterns. For these reasons marijuana is unwelcome in the modern office environment, while a drug such as coffee, which reinforces the values of industrial culture, is both welcomed and encouraged. (McKenna) It diminishes the power of the ego, has a mitigating effect on competition, causes one to question authority, and reinforces the notion of the merely relative importance of social values. (ibid)

Psychosomatic Disease

Stress-related disorders are often referred to as being psychosomatic, which is a simplified way of saying that, in the case of cancer for instance; it affects and is affected by both the body and mind. In other words, except for some cancer from environmental mishaps (as in Chernobyl or over-exposure to specific carcinogens), or in most cancers in children is a disease of, and an outgrowth from, the whole person. In such a framework, the question of responsibility for one's illness is often raised, almost as though the patient is to blame or deserves to be sick. This judgment is faulty in that it fails to appreciate the wholeness out from which a person's psychological and physiological tendencies have been forged.

Beginning with excessive conscious and unconscious interpretations of danger as a result of dysfunctional upbringing, immersion in unhealthy lifestyles, including too fast a pace of life, the wrong diet, and obsession with material success – often results in the life-sustaining systems of the entire organism becoming habitually turned away from relaxation, calmness, and expansion. Combat-ready habituation is a "whole" person agenda, most noticeably measurable as an abundance of stimulants (ANS imbalance) but also including suppression of ordinary immunological responses. Such a state defines the entire person in the same way that the totality of environmental influences is measured (with a good degree of accuracy) by scores on IQ tests. Surely no responsibility or blame can be ascribed. With the introduction of awareness into the equation, however, the possibility develops for mastering one's previously uncontrollable and damaging circumstance. In the case of cancer-prone people, who usually maintain a suspicious attitude (at least on the unconscious level) more consistently than others, the disease presents at the point in time when the body's balancing apparatus is overwhelmed, resulting in toxicity at the cellular level. Cancer cells are produced in this milieu, and reproduced at an alarming rate, since the system's defenses are degraded. The organism contracts and is unable to ward off or eliminate internal predators, e.g., bacteria, virus, poisons, cancer cells. What seems to be happening is, as the outer possibility for danger is constantly guarded against, the inner guard is compromised. Without its natural protection (of the immune system) a *vicious toxic cycle* (VTC as coined by Wallace), ensues.

Traditional medicine addresses the deranged cancer cells, and in spite of the organism's weakened state, its strategy is to eliminate the expression (cancer) of the problem by surgery, chemotherapy or radiation. This symptom- oriented medicine often fails, since the root cause of a less-than-fully-oxygenated-organism has not been eliminated (or even identified). We must also note that aggressive, conventional methods tend to exacerbate the organism's contraction, first by the dreaded connotation that attends the diagnosis of cancer, second by the fear of the horrific medical procedures used, and finally by the shock that all surgery, chemotherapy, and radiation produces on the human system.

Gentler, holistic remedies, on the other hand, address the problem at its origin, attempting to intervene on the VTC without further stressing the person. Unhealthy negative attitudes are substituted for the "imagery" of a positive nature. Strengthening the body through a detoxifying diet is a major goal, and deep breathing exercises that allow for elimination of unconscious conflict are initiated – all of which call for conscious patient participation.

> Cancer patients repress and deny unpleasant effects, such as, depression, anxiety, guilt to a significantly higher degree than do the controlled subjects. Impaired emotional outlets are significantly pronounced in lung cancer patients. (Achterberg)

The strategy is to reawaken the innate tendency to healing through rebalancing all the systems of the person. Humor also has been publicly recognized as a healing tool, over the last decade, with publication of the book *Anatomy of An Illness Perceived by the Patient* in which Norman Cousin recounts how he recovered from cancer by watching old movies of the Three Stooges and laughing his head off.

For a serious psychosomatic disease such as cancer, the benefits to be derived from marijuana cannot be overstated:

1.   The causal element of unconscious (repressed) pain is exposed.

2. The breath can be restored to fullness, thereby eliminating directly the built up toxicity and the same time, enjoining balance throughout the whole organism. A depressed system is a weakened system, and since it works holistically, marijuana gives strength where weakness exists, and expansion and relaxation where there is contraction and nervousness.
3. The more richly oxygenated blood that is in effect with marijuana can help to cleanse the poisons at the cellular level.
4. And a broader perspective through activation of the entire brain leads to positive feelings and thus eliminates the usual and debilitating attitudes so common in cancer – helplessness, depression, fear, resignation, and dread.

Application of Marijuana

Today most people associate marijuana as a material for smoking in a cigarette or a pipe, but in ancient India and in the medical profession of the Western world, marijuana has mostly been utilized in liquid forms. Bhang is the preparation of the leaves and flowers in a milk-based substance that is hailed throughout the ancient texts of the Hindus, and used as well up to the present time in India. Tincture of Cannabis was the main prescription of the Western physician (before prohibition) and was often utilized as a tonic, in addition to being prescribed for specific medicinal problems. These methods of application eliminate any worry concerning carcinogenic substances that are suggested as a by-product of marijuana smoking.

However, with the modern acceptance of medical marijuana, the vaporizer has come into favor. Rather than taking in all of the compounds of Cannabis (some of which are considered without benefit and harmful when oxygenated), the vaporizer heats the plant material just high enough to release the cannabinoids which are then delivered to the patient without smoke. There is no problem whatsoever with this new technology as far as any carcinogenic intake is concerned. This method of delivery is utilized in the progressive states where marijuana as medicine is legal as well as throughout the world for its safety and ease of application. In addition, self-titration by the patient is also facilitated with vaporization.

As for the Tincture of Marijuana which was so popular in the 19th and early 20th century, it is made from potent buds and "over 100 "proof" alcohol. Measurements of 1 pint of alcohol to 1 ounce of bud are common. After two weeks of darkness, during which time the mixture of alcohol and marijuana is shaken on a daily basis, the plant material is strained from the alcohol (leaving the tincture). It is administered in minute doses, because of its potency. If we look into the homeopathic Materia Medica(s) of the past, tincture of Cannabis is the usual form of prescription.

The allegation that smoking marijuana may cause cancer and other lung problems, however, has been shown to be baseless. The first study that suggested the harmlessness of marijuana therapy was conducted in Costa Rica. It was found that chronic marijuana smokers, who also smoked tobacco cigarettes, were less likely to develop cancer than those who didn't employ marijuana at all. Further studies have disproved all of the fears of marijuana and cancer. The latest research was suggestive of marijuana even inhibiting lung cancer, although so far those results are only preliminary. Further testing is planned which will surely validate marijuana's cancer-preventive features. So far, what is definite, however, is that marijuana is not causative to cancer. Since marijuana (by vaporization, smoking, ingestion, drinking and nowadays even a skin patch, salve or spritz under the tongue) dilates the alveoli, it is more than likely that the use of Cannabis neutralizes, or even overwhelms the constriction, by its own tendency to dilation. Marijuana via vaporization or smoking is especially efficacious in cases of severe nausea, where there is the problem of taking medicine by mouth in patients who cannot "keep anything down" (Morgan).

As an aid for all psychosomatic disease, marijuana can benefit the participant, generally because of its health-restoring effects and calming of the nervous system. Ironically, psychosomatic disease is fear expressed in its most potent form, while marijuana is feared because it will allow for the expression of fear in a more diffused and therefore less deadly fashion. The apprehension that marijuana could infiltrate into the mainstream medical arena stems from the fact that marijuana has limitless potential for treating illness. The pharmaceutical industry and the medical monopoly would lose billions of dollars if this natural plant's healing qualities become as wide-spread as its benefits would mandate.

Marijuana is incredibly useful for chemotherapy patients, yet it is not allowed by the U.S. government. Rumor has it, however, that physicians often inform their suffering patients of marijuana's therapeutic effects and suggest that they obtain a dose on the illegal market. This is especially true in the V.A. Hospitals, where chronic pain and boredom plague former soldiers and their long stays result in doctor-patient friendships, especially true in AIDS and cancer chemotherapy patients.

In the 90s, in blatant disregard of federal prohibition, Cannabis Buyers Clubs (CBC) formed to aid patients with grave and terminal illness. The clubs distribute marijuana to fill the void created by federal law. In California, the clubs have operated quite efficiently under the auspices of the 1996 Compassionate Use Law for over a decade. On occasion federal DEA official raids have been carried out against them confiscating medicine and property and prosecuting the owners. Despite the laws, almost every major city has a CBC, and for the most part, there is little enforcement of the law.

Because "chemo" poisons the system in its attempt to destroy cancer cells, the entire organism is thrown into a state of gross disequilibrium during chemotherapy. In these acute situations, Marijuana Therapy is the re-stabilizer of fast action! Patients feel better almost immediately, after just one puff. In addition, they feel better for longer periods and they feel more alert without having to take a drug. Once the chemically-induced nausea is eliminated, chemo-therapy patients often even experience a desire to eat, unthinkable only moments before administering marijuana.

In fact, enhancement of appetite has a far greater meaning than just being able to eat. A person who feels well enough to ingest take food is re-affirming life. The benefit may be seen only in the lunch taken, but the truth is that marijuana acts on the whole person. While the appetite is restored, the depressed system is re-balanced, which includes broadening the mental outlook.

A RECIPE for Bhang with Spices:

- Milk (quart) and sugar (to taste).
- Dried marijuana leaves and flowers (approximately 10 grams).
- Poppy seeds, pepper, dry ginger, caraway seeds, cloves, cinnamon, nutmeg (all according to taste).

Boil vegetation in water for 5 minutes, mash/mush as it boils. Strain and discard liquid. This can be done a few times to cut back on astringent taste. Remaining plant material, milk, and seasoning to taste is to be simmered slowly for 20 minutes. Strain liquid well, discard plant material (carefully – it is potent), add sugar. Color is greenish. Refrigerate. (Mixture for 2 men in one day*) or (1 woman for 2 days)

*Recipe according to Indian Government: to help laborers to work in the heat. Excerpted from the Indian Hemps Drugs' Commission Report.

Marijuana: Limitless Remedial Action

Once we realize the general principle by which it affects the human system, the potential medical remedies of this "most useful plant" are endless. This can be perhaps most dramatically documented with a list of recommended applications of marijuana for various illnesses, derived from Ancient Uses of Marijuana (McKenna). It was prescribed for: *malaria, beriberi, constipation, rheumatic pain, absentmindedness, female disorders, dysentery, leprosy, dandruff, headache, mania, venereal disease, whooping cough, earache, tuberculosis, snake bite, nodes/tumors, jaundice, glaucoma, asthma, muscular dystrophy, epilepsy, and excitability.* It was used to *quicken the mind, prolong life, improve judgment, lower fever, induce sleep, aid the bile, stimulate appetite, aid in child birth, and better the voice. It was known as an anti-phlegmatic, analgesic, mild sedative, tonic, anti-nauseant, and a digestive aid.*

In 19th century medicine, tincture of Cannabis was used mostly as a sedative and antispasmodic for Insomnia, migraine, epilepsy, excitability, childbirth, and menstrual discomfort. Interestingly enough, the medical reports from that time make little or no mention of psychoactive effects. People's expectations were different. Either they did not get high from it because they didn't expect to, or if they did, they paid it no attention and did not mention it to their doctors. (Weil)

If the claims that marijuana is generally beneficial are true, it follows that its regular administration may help prevent many illnesses. And it can be suggested that people otherwise predisposed to psychosomatic diseases (through mental/physical or lifestyle orientation), who have employed marijuana on a regular basis over a long period of time, will represent a much smaller percentage among the already afflicted than is true of the population-at-large. If this is the case, it would certainly rank marijuana among the most useful of preventive remedies. Whether a scientific study of this nature can be reasonably undertaken is another matter.

Divine Vision
by Joan Bello

In the cycle, unending of growth and pain
Toward the circle's bending to goodness again
The time returns to stand apart
It's come once more to stalk the heart
We have become a complex decay
A simple flower saves the day

The spark of the seed is holy and pure
The sight in the weed is offered for cure

As the spirit within the dove
Marijuana offers love
Be a temple, use the tools
Truth and flowers are God's jewels

Divine Vision personified
In a plant, simplified
With our reason nullified
By our laws crucified

Chapter 4 • Spiritual Benefits
The Third Dimension

It is relatively easy to demonstrate that marijuana is healthy for the body, since its physiological benefits can be tested objectively as well as subjectively by marijuana users. Psychological stability, although not quite so readily measurable, depends on integration between the conscious and unconscious flow of ideas. Again, the effect of marijuana corresponds to the acceptable framework of healthy awareness. However, when we address the benefits of marijuana upon the inner fabric of humanness, we begin to tread on thin ice. Since this inner world cannot be seen or measured, the materialistic perspective tends to ignore its existence.

In many societies, experimentation with growth beyond an effective ego is not encouraged. In fact, if it involves an investment of energy that detracts even temporarily from one's material productivity, it may be actually discouraged. Investing time or energy into developing oneself beyond the ego level may be better understood or appreciated by a society where economic success and material possessions are not the major criteria by which one is judged. Experimentation with higher states of consciousness may be regarded with suspicion or considered wasteful nonsense. (Ajaya)

In the area of private values, marijuana may offer benefits beyond the personal ego, which reach the dimension referred to by mystics and saints as the ever-present "now." The experience addresses states of consciousness not common to the common man and resembles Maslow's "peak experience." Rather than being a concrete, stable reality, this realm approaches intuition and ecstasy; it apprehends an unusual connectedness with the whole of life. Daily existence becomes but an invisible script where what matters is the attitude by which one lives. In the world of thought and relationship, honesty and compassion are the prime motivators, while material gain and loss are secondary. This is really an ascension to religious values; not familiar or even welcomed within the context of modern society, but certainly containing great benefit for individual happiness. Our culture has become anti-religious. Our society is based on getting, not giving, and even though our words uphold virtue and love as worthy goals, hardly anyone even tries to live by such a philosophy. The regular use of marijuana, however, can often set the stage for receptivity to this higher knowledge / level of being.

Higher Consciousness

To ascend the ladder of consciousness, human beings need as much help as they can get. Levels of consciousness above concerns of personal survival' and power are neither necessary for human life, nor visible from ordinary states. Because these higher degrees of awareness threaten the power structure, all paths to them are often outlawed. If we are not taught by some older, wiser person that deep and timeless perceptions really exist (or unless we ourselves fortuitously catch a glimpse of these subjective realities), we remain ignorant of their existence and are easily molded into the lower social goals of materialism, competition, and power. This less enlightened state is expressed by a constant gnawing dissatisfaction. It is the dimension of perennial desire. With each fulfillment of a goal/need/want, another void erupts. In Buddhism, it is the realm of nightmarish, Insatiable hunger, which cannot be resolved unless or until the being-hood attains to a less self-centered level. Deep within each of us, an essential need for a higher meaning of life waits to be awakened. Because of its ability to unlock this yearning and allow us a glimpse of the deeper reality, marijuana is feared by the establishment 'and loved by the user. Speaking about the personality change that some people undergo as a result of introduction to Cannabis, Inglis says:

> (it) does not intoxicate.... is not addictive...But (it) confronts society with an issue that it has been unwilling to face. People may need (it) not for (itself) but as a preliminary to restoration of the link, largely lost, between man's (and woman's) consciousness, and all that lies beyond. The personality change may be for their benefit.

Quoting from the LA Daim Committee, he continues:

> The positive values people find in the... experience bears a striking similarity to traditional religious values, including the concern with soul or inner self. The spirit of renunciation, the emphasis on openness and the closely-knit community are part of it, but this is definitely a sense of identification with something larger, something to which one belongs as part of the human race. (ibid)

It is mainly because spiritual values are abandoned during eras of materialism that marijuana is banned today. And, ironically, it is because these values are so absent in the modern culture that the *marijuana experience* is so ardently sought.

> Despite all the pressures brought against it, Cannabis use rose until today...(it)...may well be America's single largest agricultural

> product...the innate drive to restore the psychological balance typifying (a) partnership society, once it finds a suitable vehicle, is not easily deterred. (McKenna)

The regular use of marijuana is a sane attempt at adaptation that occurs spontaneously among certain marginal members of a group. Without an "evolutionary leap" in human priorities, the danger of extinction is real. Evolution for human beings is toward an expansion of consciousness, or cooperation, in response to present-day alienation.

The Science of Vibration

Thousands of years ago, in a non-hostile climate, known today as the cradle of civilization, marijuana was used extensively. Out from this Eden-like existence, a profound spiritual cosmology developed. "The Science of Vibration" is as valid today as it was then, but progression to our modern lifestyle (and away from finer values) excluded interest in it. Only in the last few decades has the industrialized world paid it any serious attention. Perhaps investigation into the higher human values could not surface in the industrial West until all imaginable physical, psychological, and social dysfunction reached dangerous proportions. Perhaps the further a culture falls from recognizing the realm of the sacred; the more need to exist for it to do so. Whatever the explanation, whatever the impetus, there can be no doubt of the interest that exists today concerning higher consciousness. This interest represents a dynamic tension pulling against the material ethic, for which marijuana has served as an abiding ally.

In the Eastern sciences, the vibrational makeup of creation is evidenced not only in the cosmos, but also through the human form, which is recognized as a miniature representation of the universe. Whatever principles apply to the macrocosm and its processes apply equally to the functioning of human life. With this logic, and with extensive personal experimentation, it has been discovered that the human body has a containment of powerful energy polarized along the spinal column, divided into a dynamic negative charge (at the base of the spine) and a static positive charge (at the crown of the head) - very much in keeping with the magnetism and repulsion of electromagnetic fields. Only a minuscule percentage of the total charge is used to maintain the organism, leaving a vast surplus of potential energy untapped. To trigger this dormant energy - to transverse the entire spinal pathway - stands as the highest goal of life in Eastern philosophy. With such a release, likened to the "nuclear energy of the psycho/physical system" (Saraswati), the human being is said to fulfill his/her potential.

The ascent of this charge follows the vertical column within the spine in much the same way that electricity is born along a lightening rod. As it flows upward, with the speed of light, it passes through intricate electromagnetic centers of the body that result from congested intersections of major nerves and organs. These centers are called "chakras" in the East, and they correspond to modes of behavior or levels of understanding. Although they are not visible, the chakras' fields of energetic congestion are measurable and, in the West, are just beginning to be investigated. Weil and Rosen, pioneers of Western Holistic Medicine, explain it this way:

(Yogic thinking has long recognized the two modes of the mind.)

> The brain has two major modes or systems, which must work together and be harmonized if we are not to lose the essentials of our human existence. Unfortunately, few of us are really balanced and most of us, especially men, tend towards the purely external, materialistic and technological...side rather than the subtle, intuitive, feeling side... Most of us fluctuate, according to our inner biological rhythms, moving from left to right brain, right to left nostril, active to receptive mode... From the yogic point of view, this rhythmic, or in the case of disease, arrhythmic swings, indicate that we are unbalanced and that one mode, one side of our nature is constantly becoming predominant. We rarely experience the more desirable state in which both sides become equal and balanced. According to yoga, when both the sad (left) and happy (right) hemispheres are balanced for a certain length of time, a new state arises which unites logic and intuition, transforms our emotions and enables us to power a greater range of neurological activity. (ibid)

The Christian mystic, de Chardin, explaining this same process, says "physical energy must be mastered and grounded for spiritual energy to move, because physical energy transforms the spirit" (Ferguson). Within the deep recesses of human understanding, the intuitive faculty steers its course. For many, in touch with this sixth sense, the realm of the spirit is supreme. Anything that demonstrates a possibility for psycho/spiritual uplifting is known to be sacred. Marijuana is so recognized and revered as quoted from Indian Hemp Drugs Commission:

> "Bhang brings union with the Divine Spirit."

Evolution of a person is demarcated by stages in all esoteric teachings. "The Theory of Vibration" is a seven-fold ascension that originates in the lowest human emotion of instinctive survival, situated at the base of the spine, and rises to the highest experience of pure awareness, above the crown of the head (as a halo). Seven is a mystical number in all esoteric religions, as it represents the stages of possible human evolution. Its meaning has, for the most part, been forgotten. In this model, each level of psycho-spiritual evolvement has a corresponding energetic density and a geographical site ("chakra") in the body. Every person displays a certain attitude, a predominant way of perceiving both inner and outer worlds, and also a type of action depending upon his/her stage of evolution. At the lower levels, which Freud studied extensively, there is an animal-like nature ("id") that is concerned solely with personal survival. This is an accurate account of the qualities of the low, second "level" (chakra) attitude. Freud's investigations were not concerned with demonstrating the evolutionary possibilities of humanness. His patients were limited by their extreme pathologies, and his own intellectual model did not envision development beyond an ego, driven always - only by primal desire.

Conscience

With marijuana, we uncover the unconscious creative understanding that is usually hidden, since as we have seen, right brain energizing brings an expansion in awareness (or witness). It is not the right hemisphere's increased activity alone that expands awareness. It is the balancing mode that is born with additional activity in the right hemisphere -responsible for heightened consciousness.

Balance is the state of human development from which the "objective witness" is born. It implies harmony in all areas of life, with continuous movement toward the fullness of human potential. The difference between consciousness with a 'witness' and ordinary consciousness is none other than the difference between operating with a conscience or without one. In ordinary life, we are all bound by Freud's superego, which maintains our behavior according to the social ideals we have been taught. This is the (internalized) repressive element of civilization, which restrains our animal natures from actions considered harmful to society, our church, our parents, and our peers. Without it, normal social life could not continue.

The Ten Commandments were presented to a social group that no longer functioned conscientiously and therefore needed mandatory direction. Within the deeper levels of human nature, however, an objective, timeless, universal sense of right and wrong exists. This is conscience. Unfortunately, the rules of our world are far removed from this inherent, eternal, inner understanding of right action. Our internal nature can know, but our imbalanced way of life does not allow for its fruition. From a vibrational perspective this can be understood as a lack of energy, excessive resistance, or low charge – all due to disharmony. Through balance, over time and with sincere interest, marijuana can enliven the "Center of Knowing." In the Theory of Vibration, this is the sixth level of development known as the "Knowledge Center." What we refer to as the sixth sense, or intuition, derives from this esoteric symbol, which very often is depicted as a third eye, located at the mid brow:

> ...where the mind perceives knowledge directly, via a sixth or intuitive sense, which comes into operation as the sixth (knowledge) chakra awakens...where one becomes the detached observer of all events, including those within the body and mind....often, the experience one has when awakening takes place in the Ajna Chakra (Knowledge Center) is similar to that induced by marijuana. (Saraswati)

Jesus Christ referred to this very same awakening that is evidenced within the body:

> "If therefore thine eye be single, thy
> whole body shall be full of light." (Matthew 6:22)

Consequences of Conscience

As we have seen, many an argument against marijuana refers to the non-competitive nature it engenders. During the Vietnam War, one of the major problems of our soldiers was their inability to accept the brutality of their own actions. Our young men encountered marijuana at every turn in Asia (the Vietnam War was the beginning of marijuana use in this country, since it was the first time a socio-economic cross-section of America was exposed to it), and their reaction was often not in keeping with the insensitivity necessary for war. Their conscience bothered them. Attaining to the higher values, such as compassion, cooperation, and consideration, is a function of balance and a threat to a militaristic society. If we all became aware of our conscience, who would be left to maintain the indifference of the social order? The more we uncover the spiritual element in our natures, the more sensitive we become. Scrooge had no conscience until he experienced the spirit. He was surely happier and healthier after his vision but not wealthier, for his conscience dictated that he share. His new-felt sensitivity did not result from rules, fear, or his superego. It overflowed joyfully as an expression of his higher state of being.

Marijuana's contribution to the developing spirit is cumulative. As bodily tensions are reduced, mental fears dissolve, clearing the way to greater in sight. But, until the direct effect (physical balance) of marijuana on the body and the attendant side effect (high) of marijuana in the mind become familiar, the alterations themselves remain the focus of interest. The "getting high" is the end in itself, rather than the understanding and insight that accrues as the changed set becomes more common. People who try marijuana and reject it do so usually because they feel uncomfortable and confused in the altered, fuller consciousness. Instead of life being safely framed by the rigidity of the societal dogma, the world becomes unfamiliarly bigger, brighter, fuller, yet less manageable, more unpredictable and full of mystery. A mind that has been bound and accustomed to a low charge or a setting without light very often finds the expansiveness of reality too highly energized. The light can be blinding and disorienting. Over time, and with regular intake, when these higher states of seeing are no longer the focal point of attention, a restructuring of values may emerge.

Holistic Framework of Body/Mind/Spirit

In the ancient philosophies there was no division between medicine, psychology, or religion. Today's conventional disciplines split the body from the mind and only grudgingly acknowledge the possibility of spirit. The medical doctor administers to the body, the psychologist to the mind, and the priest to the somewhat elusive notion of the personal soul. In contrast with these divisions, holistic health (integrating psychology, medicine and spiritual counseling) has gained a foothold in prevailing altitudes. By tapping the wisdom of ancient civilizations, and demonstrating its validity through modern techniques, a new potential for understanding human life is available to this time period. Less restriction, more tolerance, less fear, more compassion, are all qualities of higher consciousness, and often functions of long-term marijuana use.

The timeless, higher values have been submerged over the entire gamut of what is termed "modern" history (600 years or so). In their place, religious' institutions set forth regulations that serve the organizations, and the pleasure of fellowship, but hold little possibility for personal experiences of joy. The esoteric kernel of merger with the sublime has been lost and, with it, the methods to attain to full understanding. Yet, by definition, true religion strives to increase wisdom and compassion. That is why to so many, the *marijuana experience* is religious, for it allows for a more meaningful assessment of the whole of life when unstable elements of the personality are resolved.

All experience, say the mystics, is but one piece of an infinite puzzle. Science continually discovers a piece at a time. This modern practice overlooks the forest for the trees. The cooperation of body, mind and spirit is the ultimate holistic framework of human potential, but generally escapes our modern, materialistic minds. Marijuana, an ancient plant used for thousands of years, throughout ancient civilizations to benefit this integration, is being used today for this very same reason by persons who love the effect it has on them and their lives, without exactly understanding its operation. Hopefully, we have lessened that ignorance.

The Question of Soul

Medicine...regards the human body as a machine. Scientists treat matter as dead and completely separate from themselves. - Capra

Modern psychology has sought to disassociate from religious beliefs.... to show itself to have a scientific attitude. – Ajaya

In order to present my holistic ideas, I almost fell into the "scientific" trap. It seemed that only by a thoroughly objective analysis of the way marijuana affects the body and the mind would I be able to impart the extensive benefits of this ancient plant. Five years ago, it became clear to me that there was much more to the explanation than just what can be measured objectively. When a well-known publisher wanted to buy the rights to The Benefits of Marijuana, if I would drop the Spiritual Chapter (which he felt might be a "turn off" to the secular mainstream), I knew in that instant the importance of the spiritual aspect of marijuana; I declined his offer. I had not addressed nearly as much as I believe concerning the mysterious Divinity that abides within marijuana.

My purpose in writing this book was to expose the long-forgotten healing qualities of marijuana; and to share the intuitive knowledge that had been bestowed upon me concerning the expansion of consciousness that occurs with its reverential use. I believe that the immortal soul orchestrates our every turn and is responsible for the workings of the body and mind. The state of being that is accessible through marijuana is a fleeting glimpse of the deepest esoteric truth. It is the seed of an even larger realization, which over time, grows toward awakening to the non-transitory spiritual underlay.

An ancient Hindu narrative demonstrates the East's seemingly limitless knowledge of the labyrinthine workings of the Universe, simultaneously demonstrating the limited breadth of the reductionistic methods of Western Materialism.

"There is a river. It flows with observable rhythm, in harmony with the Celestial Lights. The Eastern student notices this in quietude with absorbed and one-pointed interest. The river's existence is sustenance to all flora and fauna in its path – all of which the student scrutinizes and registers to memory. The tributaries of the river give life to the crops and allow for the continuation of the (past and present) groupings of

civilization, as well as all domesticated and wild animals, all flowers and edible vegetation. The student studies how and when the river ebbs and flows, down to its minuscule cause and effect (without motive to control this natural process). Because of innate curiosity to understand the Cause of All, the seeker investigates in earnest. The search is slow and takes total concentration. Ever-higher levels are accessed. The higher the ascent up the mountain, the finer, purer (or in other words more simple and predictable), everything becomes.

Less baggage may be carried as one ascends to the next higher plateau. Less dense forms of eating, thinking and breathing are natural to this learning process. Perceptions become clear since less diversions abound as the climb continues to The Single Source.

After endless climbing, the serous seeker reaches the mountain top, from which springs the river in endless profusion. This is the moment of realization! the attainment of yogic satisfaction, the level of the Third Eye where the individual soul knows itself in direct relationship to the Mystery (body and mind having been purified and are no longer hindrances - the goal of yoga).

Atop the rock, sits a Western scientist, having arrived (typically) by helicopter, without benefit of noticing any of the precise workings of the eternal flow. He carries much baggage (apparel and apparatus to aid in breathing the thin air not having gotten accustomed to such fine oxygen over time, and also electronic devices and modern communication tools as well). The scientist plans to tap the Source for profit. S/he notices the yogi(ni), without almost all baggage, attire, and even food stuff, sitting in idle and blissful oblivion.

The scientist asks the typical question that mechanically springs to a grasping, information-filled head: "Why and how does the water flow?" Astonished that such a question is being asked, The yogi(ni) departs from silence – "Thou are That" which quite predictably is of contemptible disinterest to the scientist.

It serves the listener to realize that the Source is mysterious, to be known and appreciated (not challenged or changed) as the Blessedness It is. This "knowing" is the level of Marijuana as Sacrament, where the individual soul is intuitively aided in realization of the Divine by the inherent vibration within the plant.

The ultimate state of consciousness in Eastern philosophy is realizing one's own true essence as identical with the illimitable, immortal consciousness: Existence, Knowledge, and Bliss ("Sat, Chit, Ananda").

By the grace of the Mystery and through the receptiveness of no division ("advaita") and absolutely not under the control of the seeker, the aspirant's consciousness enters the realm of Unity – joining with the ocean of Unitary Consciousness as all separate waves ultimately do - so that the "observer and observed are one" (Krishnamurti).

The moral of the story: Growth in knowledge is self-sustaining if preconceived notions and self-serving motives are discarded (symbolic of yogic purification). All aids to such purification are valid. According to Tantra - the East's most profound religious thought - any method for un-coupling from one's baggage is to be embraced, even worshipped. The *Hemp* is one such Holy Aid.

In truth, it is the soul that is impacted most prominently with marijuana, and all the intricate, measurable, observable, and subjective bodily and mental effects that I have explained so carefully (and so carefully admitting of no such directorship) are secondary to the conscious impact and omniscience of the Source that may be imparted to the true seeker by the mystery within the marijuana plant.

Over the course of human cultures since the beginning of recorded history, marijuana has been recognized and revered, and periodically suppressed and disrespected. At this moment in time, specifically in proactive response to the dark forces that denigrate the *marijuana consciousness*, there has once again emerged a formalized, collective appreciation of the vibrational luminescence within the plant.

To Save your Soul
by Joan Bello

Do you smoke the weed
Do you know its treasure
Do you save the seed
To grow yourself more pleasure
Then I can talk to you
And you to me
For you are one of those
Who always wants to see
That this life without a goal
Makes you want to cry
So you smoke – To save your soul
And help your spirit fly

"First Cannabis High?"

Dr. Grinspoon was the "voice of reason," during decades of marijuana demonization. As the Medical Expert for the Class Action Lawsuit, he was refreshingly down to earth, very knowledgeable and always helpful. But I never suspected that he was a marijuana person.

"It seemed like a very long time before we arrived home. Not that we were in a rush -- the ride was very pleasant. Time passed even more slowly between our arrival and our going to bed, but once we did, we knew with certainty that we had finally been able to achieve a marijuana high. And that marked the beginning of …my Cannabis era."

"I was 44 years old in 1972 when I experienced this first marijuana high. Because I have found it both so useful and benign I have used it ever since…as a recreational drug, as a medicine, and as an enhancer of some capacities….It has been so useful that I cannot help but wonder how much difference it would have made had I begun to use it at a younger age….it has been so helpful in arriving at some important decisions and understandings, it is tempting to think that it might have helped me to avoid some "before Cannabis era" bad decisions."

"I cannot possibly convey the breadth of things it helps me to appreciate, to think about, to gain new insights into…On those evenings when I smoke marijuana it provides, among other things, an invitation to review significant ideas, events and interactions of the day."

"Currently…there are two generic categories of marijuana use: recreational and medical…(but) many uses fall into a third category that I call enhancement: (including) magnification of pleasure in a host of activities ranging from dining to sex, increased ability to hear music and see works of art, and the ways in which it appears to catalyze new ideas, insights and creativity."

(from "A Cannabis Odyssey," Lester Grinspoon, M.D.)

Chapter 5 • The Eastern Understanding

I was very lucky to receive a rigorous and non-conventional Graduate course of study, under the direct guidance of an advanced yogi, specifically to prepare me "to be a bridge" between the ancient Eastern wisdom and modern Western science. I never knew how that awesome mission would unfold, but with my research with Cannabis over the last decade I have learned.

The teaching professors for the Graduate course were practicing doctors and licensed psychologists from highly-acclaimed universities: Harvard/ Duke/Chicago/Buffalo, or equally prestigious Oriental schools. The students as well as the American faculty had all gravitated to the precise and extensive knowledge of the immense body of thought, known as Indian Philosophy, out of a deep-felt need that Western "science" could not satisfy. Originally I came to the facility because it was instrumental in curing my son of epilepsy. When a Master's in Science Degree at the Institute was offered, there was no doubt in my mind that it was the training I needed.

The Indian tradition spans 5000 years of accumulated knowledge, under which the sciences of religion, psychology, and medicine are interdependent and completely compatible; its depth of understanding flew in the face of modern belief systems and was vastly superior to them. In Ayurveda (traditional Indian medicine) the physician is responsible for guiding the student to "full spiritual integration with the universe" - considered the only worthy goal of human existence. This requires, first of all, health of body and mind, which is understood as a progressive, intentional purification process. Throughout the history of India, the Cannabis plant has played a major role for: growth in the spirit, peace of the mind, and medicine for the body, not to mention the myriad industrial uses which it served for millennia.

During my formal studies, Marijuana Therapy was not discussed at all owing to its taboo in modern American culture. But the extensive private research library was full with treasures of Eastern medical tomes and "Oriental Studies' Journals" which gave Cannabis its rightful place in health and attainment to higher consciousness. This library was where I spent most of my time during the five years that I was a student. I began collecting and studying these books and journals voraciously.

Occasionally, I took courage to question the doctors about the effect of the herb. It always elicited the same response: *a unique sedative-stimulant*. The Subject would end in an awkward silence that I was understandably afraid to pursue.

Since, in the Eastern framework, a balanced Autonomic Nervous System is health" as well as a prerequisite for realization of the highest truth, all practice (diet/yoga/meditation) was toward that end. The student body was very small and we were painstakingly trained as scientific experimenters, acknowledging and recording our experiential reactions, as well as the objective, more – easily measured responses of the body. Subjective reality is without merit in the West, but the Eastern tradition considers it of utmost importance. Through all of the experimentation, the goal was to become totally alert, while completely at ease, a state that can be translated as a dynamic tension between excitation and relaxation or "sedation/stimulation." All my free time was spent researching the unique hemp plant which had become very important in my life. I was not introduced to it until I was nearly 30 years old. Perhaps this fact played a major role in the impelling impact it had on my consciousness. Perhaps there is a more esoteric explanation for my one-pointed interest. Whatever the reason - I was avidly curious to prove what I suspected: that marijuana stabilizes the unconscious, automatic reactions of the human organism. Most of my fellow students acknowledged that Cannabis enhanced mental faculties and physical well-being, but I was alone in my zealousness to learn just how it worked.

From one of our more outspoken American professors, the mystery of the ecstasy gained with LSD was revealed as a "flooding of both sides of the ANS." He explained that it mimicked the orgasmic reaction and was similar to the state attained in the highest consciousness, where the bliss of life is manifest. From that gem of information, in conjunction with the Science of Breath, and the accumulations of my research, I began to piece together the unrealized balancing ability of marijuana on the ANS. There was also one other important factor that spurred me on in my research - my son's epilepsy.

Although they were careful never to proselytize the benefits of marijuana, the actions of the holistic doctors belied their silence. About 10 years before I became a student, my 11- year - old son was a patient at the Homeopathic Clinic. I took him there in a desperate attempt to find a cure for his progressively worsening epilepsy. Conventional medical treatment had not helped him (despite prescriptions of increasingly aggressive drugs). Being the mischievous child that he was, during his weekly outpatient visit, my young son would confide to his assigned doctors (there were three of them) that he smoked marijuana regularly and with my knowledge. I would sit quietly in the corner, trying to melt into the walls, but unable to admonish him, because I knew that holistic treatment required total honesty. The oddest part of the story is that not one of his doctors ever admonished him either. At the end of each weekly hour-long session, they would always remind us both: "no potato chips, no meat, and no antibiotic medication." Whenever he became ill, my husband and I would take him to the clinic for a "remedy" that usually worked - seemingly miraculously - in 24 hours. After six months of intensive holistic health practice, biofeedback training, appropriate homeopathic remedies, and continuous meetings with Swami Rama, my son was cured. That was 30 years ago.

Needless to say, I am forever grateful. His cure, along with the silent sanctioning of his regular use of Cannabis, is the reason I became a student of Eastern Science and was charged with the awesome responsibility of serving as a bridge between the East and the West. With the completion of this work, I feel somewhat relieved of that mandate but I also know that my work in the field of Marijuana Therapy is not yet finished.

Viewpoints: East and West

In defining Holistic Health, holistic refers to the whole person: body, mind and spirit; health is the harmonious interplay of these three levels of human life. Whereas lost equilibrium manifests itself as disease!

Modern Western medicine would not question anything so obviously true, but neither would it be interested in it. First of all, a three-dimensional model of human life is beyond the framework of Twentieth Century Science which focuses almost exclusively on the physical, as a natural consequence of cultural materialism. In such an agenda, only what we can own, see, taste and touch is valued. The underlying cause for the physical manifestation is not considered. The notion that automatic body processes are coordinated by an invisible component is meaningless from such an "objective scientific" approach. Although the medical profession never denies the existence of a life force, no serious study of the magnitude of its input on health is addressed. The Eastern Understanding that full health implies interconnected harmony of the physical, mental, and spiritual realms of human life manifesting as a dynamic balance of the Autonomic Nervous System has not been studied in the West, nor is there any reason to believe it will be in the near future. To do so, would require a total revolution both philosophically and economically, since conventional therapy today is so heavily invested (on all levels) in an aggressive path of research for external management of disease symptoms. In the Western model, the doctor is the authority and the patient follows instructions. Illness is inflicted on the afflicted from the outside. Instead, in the ancient holistic Ayurvedic Tradition, illness is an expression of the disharmony from within. Treatment is a determined and joint investigation of the root cause by both the student and the teacher, an endeavor which will ultimately result in a purposeful change in behavior.

The sad fact is that disciplined, self-regulated change is not part of the educational repertoire of our culture. A secular society, disinterested in the underlying nature of reality, and correspondingly indifferent to the possibility that regulating behavior can help prevent disease, cannot embrace the basic tenets of Holistic Health.

As it is not proper to try - to cure the eyes without the head, nor the head without the body, so neither is it proper to cure the body without the soul, and this is the reason why so many diseases escape (Greek) physicians who are ignorant of the whole. (Plato)

From that timeless 3000 year old quote, we can see that the problem of lifestyle causing sickness has not really changed, and that, in general, the 'physicians' outlook has maintained its narrow focus.

So you think our medicine is primitive?

That's the wrong word. It isn't primitive. It's fifty percent terrific and fifty percent nonexistent. Marvelous antibiotics – but absolutely no methods for increasing resistance, so that antibiotics are not needed. Fantastic operations - but when it comes to teaching people the way of going through life without having to be chopped up – absolutely nothing. Apart from sewage systems and synthetic vitamins, you don't seem to do anything at all about prevention and yet you have a proverb: "prevention is better than cure." - Aldous Huxley

In those areas where technique and machines can x-ray a fracture, help the precision of operations, and maybe soon, perform operations with greater precision than even the best of surgeons, and including all the incredible emergency medical procedures that have been developed in the last century, Western Medicine has made boundless and unequalled strides. In the area of internal disharmony (the natural consequence of habits that are unhealthy but nevertheless widespread), the ancient understanding is undeniably superior.

Historical Uses for Cannabis

Down through the centuries in nearly all kinds of cultures throughout the entire world, Cannabis has been acknowledged as a unique and invaluable regulator, if not a "gift of the gods."

From the Medicinal Plants of India & Pakistan, Cannabis is listed as "bhang, charas, ganja, hashish, subzee, vijaya." Every part of this wondrous plant was used for numerous ailments.

The leaves are sensitive, anodyne, narcotic, antispasmodic, diuretic, digestive and astringent; as a sedative and anodyne they are given in doses of 40 grains; in dysentery and diarrhea half a drachm of the dried leaves are given with sugar and black pepper; the leaves are administered to induce sleep where opium cannot be used; they are also used in tetanus and dysmenorrhoea. A paste of the fresh leaves is used to resolve tumors; their juice removes dandruff and head lice; their powder is a useful dressing for wounds and sores; a poultice of the leaves is applied to the eyes in ophthalmia and other diseases, and to piles.

The preparation made from specially dried leaves and flowers, known as bhang or hashish, is given in dyspepsia, gonorrhea and bowel complaints and as appetizer and nervine stimulant.

The dried pistillate flowering tops, coated with a resinous exudation are known as ganja; the smoke from burning ganja is swallowed as an antidote to poisoning. The smoke is passed through the rectum for relief of strangulated hernia and gripping pains of dysentery. It is given in one-fourth to two grain doses.

This latter, anal remedy, leaves us to wonder about the other receptors, not connected with the hypothalamus, that exist on the surfaces of, and within internal organs of, our bodies. Receptors recently discovered and published in scientific journals only touch on this idea.

Charas, the resinous exudation that collects on the leaves....is of great value in malarial and periodic headaches, migraine, acute mania, insanity, delirium. whooping cough...asthma, anemia of brain, nervous vomiting, tetanus, convulsions, nervous exhaustion and dysuria; it is also used as an anesthetic in dysmenorrheal, as an appetizer, as an aphrodisiac...in eczema, neuralgia, severe pains, etc; it is usually given in one sixth to one fourth grain doses. The seeds are used in infusion for gonorrhea.

The author J.F. Datur makes a statement at the beginning of his book that, unfortunately, prognosticates exactly what has occurred: "with the advancement of pharmaceutical research, there is increasing exploitation of our resources. But we are uncovering the ancient truths once again - that natural marijuana is a miraculous medicine."

And from the Materia Medica by Ruddock in homeopathic treatment, Cannabis is recommended:

...for difficulty of urinating;....and menstrual headache...sometimes greatly helped; for opacity of cataract and specks on the cornea. For constipation, and in humid times, for asthma, and for the effects at alcoholic intoxication.

The following studies are based on just a tiny sampling of the already existent Western-style scientific documentation available and waiting to be integrated with the measured effects of marijuana that reveal why this primal earth medicine has enjoyed such ubiquitous, ancient and long-standing recognition. Its rediscovery by the modern world is an event whose time is at hand. Hopefully the following research will help to bridge the gap between the traditions of intuitive realization and the science of objective knowledge.

The Herb and Epilepsy

For the first 30 years of my life, my rebellious nature would occasionally show itself, but for the most part, I was mainstream mediocrity – all the way. Then, when I found the herb, all the conditioning of socialization, law-abidingness, organized religion, and social correctness lost their importance. Simplicity and honesty and kindness became ultra-significant, which o f course changed everything. I entered the realm of altered consciousness which felt magically religious. I was Alice looking out and looking in - all at once, and I recognized this feeling in the pit of my being. It was eternally familiar, but absolutely new.

I'm a serious person by nature, that didn't change. Getting high let me understand that there is always profound meaning behind the script. Most importantly, it let me be who I had always known I was, deep down, like a "conversion." It was that dramatic! I acted almost immediately to share this wonder with my son. He was six and had suffered from seizures for the past four years.

Back in the early 70's no one talked about the medicinal value of marijuana, but I knew that it would help Steven. It took a long time, nearly 5 years. He stopped taking phenol-barbital and had regular visits with Swami Rama. He was treated with homeopathy and always used pot. Slowly his hyperactivity subsided. By the time he was 11 he had no more seizures. I'm sure the Swami and the homeopathic physicians were instrumental in his cure. I'm just as sure that daily marijuana helped to set the needed tone of receptivity.

Steven is 41 now, works in the high-pressure mortgage business, still has an intense character, but never has a seizure. Like millions of people in America, he partakes of marijuana whenever the opportunity presents itself, just like my other sons: Robert, the attorney and Richard, the CFO.

Because of our love and trust in this holy herb, we have suffered religious persecution at the hands of the state. My husband served time in prison. I spent time in Jail. Our family savings went to the Criminal Injustice System. Our home has been uprooted. From afar it seems we have lost so much of value. But we keep the magic.

Alcoholism

As a Drug and Alcohol Counselor, I witnessed the devastating effects of alcoholism at close range. Unfortunately, throughout the three years that I was employed by a county agency, I can report very few long-term success stories, and my colleagues would be in total agreement. There were actually only two. Both were mothers who had lost custody of their young children owing to alcoholism. I followed their progress after the protracted battle with Social Services to regain their children and was happy to find out that, even after four years, they were both free from alcohol. But their stories are the exception. Even for those clients who were entirely sober for years, either because of imprisonment or threat of imprisonment, as soon as the legal reason was gone, so was their sobriety.

The psychological problems that cause alcoholism are unconscious fears and feelings of despondency which understandably cause a strong urge to numb the mental anguish and its attendant physical nervousness. Alcohol does this quickly, surely, legally, and lethally. Once the addiction is ingrained, only an overwhelming motivation is enough reason to endure the extreme discomfort of withdrawal.

"Alcoholics Anonymous" is the only treatment modality that conventional medicine acknowledges. It works for only a select number of alcoholics, who: 1) first and foremost, desperately want to attain sobriety; 2) are able to face at least some of their hidden agenda; 3) are not adverse to the religious basis and bias of AA; and 4) can substitute coffee, confession, and camaraderie in place of alcohol. But the sad fact is that most alcoholics never really seriously try to stop drinking until it's too late and the diagnosis is grave.

After three years with the County Agency, I went into private practice. I was no longer limited by legal restrictions or fear of losing my job, I could put into practice what I had learned as a student of Holistic Health and Eastern Studies:

1. Self-Awareness and Self-Discipline are of utmost importance when regulating one's own behavior.
2. Don't bite off more than you can chew.
3. To break a bad habit, a good one must be substituted.

These three tenets are really in contradiction to the ideology underlying the AA model, which teaches alcoholics to relinquish control to a power greater than oneself and to stop all drinking immediately. In yogic psychology, we begin with gradual substitution of healthy habits. Self-awareness reigns supreme, and through it one regains control of the ability to direct one's own actions. Moderation is the message, so that total abstinence is not expected at first (as in the AA model) because it is so difficult, and ultimately results in failure, which adds to despondency. Rather than a complete, abrupt about-face from an unhealthy lifestyle, in my practice, gradual substitution of marijuana for alcohol was encouraged.

Many alcoholics use pot without realizing its therapeutic benefits. For them, the idea of increasing marijuana use while decreasing alcohol intake was not difficult. With hindsight, I realize it must have been surprising to have a counselor suggest that smoking a joint instead of drinking a beer was a good idea. The biggest problem is that most alcoholics believe that marijuana is just another bad habit. Once the truth was explained to them, and if they truly wanted to stop abusive drinking, substitution of marijuana became acceptable. I was just a catalyst for their change.

By emphasizing marijuana in place of drinking at specific times, but not at all times, many of my alcoholic clients automatically increased awareness of the reasons for desiring alcoholic stupor. Pot fulfilled the "good habit as a substitution for a bad one" requirement and it helped ease the symptoms of withdrawal, which are often insurmountable. To be honest, only three or four of my clients were able to stop drinking completely. They were all regular marijuana smokers before I knew them. If I had to do it over again, I would be much more direct. As it was, I only encouraged Marijuana as Therapy, ever so subtly.

In the framework of holistic health, alcoholism is not an incurable illness. To call it a disease is to acknowledge the extreme disequilibrium alcoholism causes for the person and the family. But in this culture, once we name something a "disease," we are expected to relinquish all control and become the obedient patient. Any personal responsibility for the disease is lifted. In the treatment of alcoholism, this disservice to the patient is magnified when the alcoholic assumes complete helplessness and hopelessness. Instead of being encouraged to change old habits through self-awareness, the medical model of conventional health care disregards the need for, and potential of, altering, at least at first, small parts of unhealthy habits and instead accepts unconsciousness as absolute and eternal. Marijuana Therapy, however, awakens us to the existence of our inner potential and allows us to sense a dimension of life that is deeper than the material.

Yoga psychology is the accumulated wisdom of thousands of years. Self-knowledge is its basic teaching. All the tools and techniques that aid in the growth of consciousness were recognized and revered long ago. Marijuana was considered a *gift of the gods* to help human life toward ever-greater understanding. Just as it worked 5000 years ago, this ancient medicine for the body, mind and spirit is working today and is being rediscovered by health care providers and patients alike.

Alcoholism has often been called the *sickness of the soul* because those who succumb are usually overly sensitive to the loss of Divine purpose in today's world. In this regard, Marijuana Therapy can help the addict regain connection with Timeless Values – if only the truth be known.

Asthma

The Holistic Model of dis-ease is actually based upon ancient philosophy (rediscovered and renamed) that human life is composed of Body, Mind and Soul. The body is only the visible representation of a whole person. The mind is the finest instrument; but the soul is the source of life. The unencumbered body and the clearest mind allow for recognition of that which abides beyond the physical and mental realities. A healthy soul is the goal of all spiritual disciplines and a requirement for the serenity sought in Holistic Health. Toward that end, the pattern of the breath is either a help or hindrance.

Our manner of breathing is consistent with our general level of health and well-being. It reflects the degree of harmony between the inner being and the outer personality. "The breath affects more than the body, for the rhythms of the body in turn affect one's emotional and mental life. In yoga science, the breath is considered to be the main link between body and mind" (Ajaya). By attaining a "pure" breath we integrate the exposed self with the secret self. Marijuana can facilitate this synthesis through its balancing effect on the Autonomic Nervous System (ANS), which regulates breathing.

Quiet, slow, sure, without ripple or pause, with depth and consistency - such a breathing pattern assures that we are centered/balanced, and at one with ourselves. In today's confounded social setting such a breath is rare. "Most people are poor breathers. Their breathing is shallow and they have a tendency to hold their breath in any situation of stress which increases tension" (Lowen). Through interest, patience, and one-pointed determination, practiced in solitude, in silent meditation, with the aid of the "sacred Bhang" the Science of Breath was formulated, in and about India over 5000 years ago by the early Hindu seekers.

Along with the stressors of modern life, breathing irregularities have escalated as evidenced by the increase of respiratory dysfunctions. The ancient traditions recognized the significance of full and unobstructed patterns of breath, whereas modern science does not. According to Dr. Andrew Weil:

> Breathing...is not information I got in medical school. I learned nothing about breathing as a bridge between mind and body, the connection between consciousness and unconsciousness, the movement of spirit in matter...(or that) breath is the master key to health and wellness...A great many teachings from such diverse

traditions as yoga, martial arts, Native American religion, natural childbirth and osteopathic medicine all point to breath as the most important function of life.

Biologically speaking, the ANS connects conscious and unconscious desires. Chronic conflict presents itself in the body as a "psychosomatic" disease, which develops over time because ANS imbalance results in either over or under secretions of body chemicals - chronically.

An asthma attack is a sudden obstruction of the airway. The bronchial tubes become so severely constricted (through contraction of the muscles that surround the bronchiole) that an asthmatic patient cannot breathe! The attack is triggered (on the physical plane) by the release of histamines from specialized cells, without the corresponding appropriate release of antihistamines. Holistic practitioners perceive that the root cause of this problem is attributable to the "asthmatic personality" (and to a lesser degree, the "allergic personality type") who habitually overreacts emotionally, but without awareness, to the point that ANS functioning is chronically, dangerously destabilized. Conventional medicine, on the other hand, perceives the symptoms as being induced by substances in the air (allergens) that affect only certain people - without the reason being of concern to allopathic doctors or, as in the psychiatric explanation, caused by repressed resentment (for which amelioration of symptoms are not specifically addressed).

Once an asthma attack begins, indicating that hidden disharmony is being expressed, additional body responses kick in, which further impairs breathing. Since stale air is trapped inside the lung and the airway is constricted, the asthmatic must forcibly expel the old gas to make room for new, oxygenated air. This severe coughing (paroxysm) takes a great deal of energy and is totally exhausting, because expiration is inherently a reaction to inspiration: air that is inhaled is automatically exhaled. Forced expiration causes the diaphragm to be pushed up (more than usual) which then pulls the ribs in closer. The frantic attempt to help oneself is instinctive, yet futile; it exacerbates the problem, for the chest cavity becomes diminished in size. The area available for expansion of the lung is decreased. At the same time, with constriction of the bronchiole, the usual upward and outward expectorant movement is constrained. Mucus buildup occurs, which further hampers the breathing process. The amount of mucus increases and becomes thicker than usual because specialized mucus-producing cells within the lung are activated during the asthmatic attack.

Epinephrine (adrenaline, a strong stimulant) inhalants are successful for suppressing the acute attack (as are injections for faster relief of symptoms). Caution is recommended as anxiety and tachycardia may result from this treatment.

Standard prophylactic treatment of asthma includes oral epinephrine (adrenaline), with possible use of sedatives to combat side effects (taken with caution so as not to depress respiration dangerously). Tranquilizers may also be prescribed on an "as needed" basis for the panic that accompanies the realization that one can have an attack at any moment. Cough medicines are also administered, but not too much, so as to avoid depressing the cough reflex. When all else fails, adreno-cortical steroids are employed which, after only a few months, can have devastating side effects:

> Steroids cause allergies and inflammation to disappear as if by magic, in fact, the magic is nothing other than direct suppression of immune function, I have no objection to giving these strong drugs for very severe or life-threatening problems, but even then I think they should be limited to short-term use. Steroids are terribly toxic, cause dependence, suppress rather than cure disease, and reduce the chance of healing by natural methods of treatment. Moreover, they weaken Immunity. (Weil).

And finally, after prolonged treatment with all of the above, drug tolerance/resistance sets in and oxygen-inhalants are life-saving. Needless to say, each progressive step to suppress bodily symptoms causes increased undesirable and unhealthy effects.

Conventional asthma treatments are delivered to the location of each symptom, the farthest point from its cause. An apt analogy would be distributing life jackets after a flood, rather than maintaining the damn site to prevent a flood in the first place. Of course, once the waters break through, life jackets save lives just as inhalers and injections, etc., save lives during an asthma attack. The person can breathe again, panic diminishes, and the body slowly begins to re-stabilize (to an increasingly skewed familiarity). But if this keeps happening - time after time - the entire infrastructure is compromised. That is to say, like the unattended damn which gives way, the integrity of all the body systems are degraded and they collapse.

Marijuana as medicine works differently in that its performance is on the ANS, the site of the origin of the asthma attack. It not only stops an attack (at its inception) but also helps prevent further attacks by consistently balancing the two sides of the ANS (Sympathetic and

Parasympathetic). Over time, it may expose the hidden psychological agendas that predispose a patient toward asthma in the first place. Marijuana affects the whole process that causes histamine overproduction at the origin of confusion, because it works on the source of the disturbance. The Hypothalamus portion of the brain directs the ANS and provides the perfect receptor-site, or "keyhole," for the THC molecule.

Marijuana Therapy is non-aggressive and non-invasive. It intercepts and reorders the life-threatening message before it is sent. It works directly at the source, and, since it is not a drug (because it has no toxicity or addictive properties, owing to its simultaneous capacity to sedate and stimulate, and is not overly concentrated by a manufacturing process), marijuana has no rebound/resistance/tolerance downside and therefore remains effective over time.

More importantly, marijuana expands lung capacity. We breathe more deeply and slowly. When taken regularly, the marijuana effect helps the lungs to retain their expanded capacity. Its efficacy does not diminish over the long term, because there is no rebound, resistance or tolerance. Marijuana affects the ANS almost immediately by causing bronchiole expansion. Histamine production is appropriately slowed or halted. Skeletal muscles in the chest are likewise relaxed through ANS mediation. The person can breathe again and peace is restored. Expectorant activation increases because marijuana improves smooth muscle motility, which moves the fluids up and out of the lung - one of the main reasons Cannabis-based cough medicine was so popular before synthetic medications replaced it at the pharmacy.

Using marijuana as a medical agent does not imply smoking; it can be ingested in other forms, such as tincture of marijuana (popular in the 19th and early 20th century). Dosage can be easily stabilized in tinctures. Modern administration for asthma, however is usually vaporization. With the development of the vaporizer, asthmatic patients are effectively medicated with no complications whatsoever. The relief is immediate with the patient in charge of dosage.

The hidden agendas within the psyche responsible for psychosomatic disease can be exposed with regular Marijuana Therapy. Over the long term, amelioration of the symptoms may very well be joined to mitigation of the root cause. (Of course, we will never know whether this is an actuality, unless studies are conducted over the long term to test this hypothesis - and made public to those whose lives could be dramatically improved.) Remember: disturbances that remain hidden cannot be dealt with, but when exposed their power to disturb is seriously diminished.

These explanations are very simplified and have not yet been verified in "scientific" experiments; although the most progressive representatives of modern medicine admit to the efficacy of Marijuana Therapy (because the results are so overwhelmingly positive). In addition, the proven myriad effects of marijuana that have been scientifically documented are indicated for asthmatic symptoms. With the increased recognition of medical marijuana in countries throughout the modern world, Cannabis-based medicines are being licensed legally and designed for fast and easy access for the patient in need of relief in a hurry. The latest attempt at marketing the *intact plant* – but as a remedy needing a doctor's prescription – is a "spritz" bottle with juiced extract from the Cannabis Sativa Plant.

Chemotherapy and Nausea

In 1995, Life Sciences released a summary of the medical studies dealing with children with cancer who had been given marijuana to relieve the nausea and vomiting associated with chemotherapy. In total, there were 480 subjects.The results were unquestionably amazingly favorable, and should have been hailed as "miraculous." It is well known that chemotherapy usually causes intense nausea, invariably followed by violent vomiting and, of course, complete loss of appetite. The Life Sciences studies reported that all 480 youngsters, ranging in age from three to thirteen, responded positively to the therapeutic administration of delta-8-tetrahydrocannabinol: "Vomiting was completely prevented. The side effects observed were negligible."

Chemotherapy is a medical euphemism for "poisoning," the rationale of which is that cancer cells multiply exceedingly rapidly and therefore tend to metabolize the poison faster than normal cells, thus being destroyed more, and more quickly, than the integrity of the entire organism - unless the poisoning happens to destroy the body or demoralize the patient past the point of affirming life. From the holistic standpoint, the rationale for poisoning the patient is completely untenable. However, conventional "wisdom" continues to employ this technique of systematically attacking the symptoms of disease rather than altering the cause or encouraging lifestyles that prevent the problem.

The substances that are used to halt or at least slow the proliferation of cancer cells (called "antineoplastic agents") are extremely toxic to the system, and understandably cause the patient to feel very sick:

> You have to understand that chemotherapy-induced nausea is "not an upset tummy. It is absolutely debilitating. I wound up curled up in a ball in the fetal position, covered with my own vomit. It is violent action. You just keep heaving and heaving....and your system just erupts - just overwhelming physical agony. (Ralph Seeley)

Common sense tells us that those who endure this treatment – especially children – ought to be afforded anything and everything that can alleviate their suffering. Dr. Grinspoon, himself, came to witness the miraculous effect it had on his son who underwent chemotherapy. With just a little bit of marijuana the nausea was gone, the desire to eat returned, and, naturally, "the spirit was lifted." The 1995 report from Life Sciences demonstrates that all children who must undergo chemotherapy may well benefit in like manner. In fact, to keep this therapy from suffering children is criminal.

The title of the article, *An Efficient New Cannabinoid Anti-emetic in Pediatric Oncology*, is somewhat of a misnomer, for Cannabis is certainly not new in the treatment of nausea and vomiting, since it was used for thousands of years by the ancient cultures. But, it is true that once again this natural remedy is being "discovered."

To understand why marijuana is perhaps the best medicine for chemotherapy - induced nausea and vomiting, we can turn again to Ralph Seeley:

> I would be getting these chemicals pumped into my veins on Friday night... Saturday and Sunday and sometimes even Monday or even Tuesday, this nausea lust comes on without warning. You're just retching and you can't stop. Legal medication is in the form of pills, which is very ineffective in a vomiting patient. You take one of the damn tablets and it just comes right back up.
>
> Now, you smoke a little marijuana, you get relief within 2-3 minutes...Secondly, you don't have to get that super dose. (Whereas) on 5 milligrams of Marinol, it makes you too high and unable to concentrate and unable to do your work... (with marijuana) you feel a little bit high, the nausea recedes...there's no hangover.

From so many testimonials, regarding so many ailments, told by people from all walks of life, in all different eras and from every country in the world, we can see that Marijuana Therapy is not just an ancient remedy prescribed by what, in our arrogance, we call "primitive" cultures. In the 18th, 19th, and early 20th century, Cannabis indica and

Cannabis Sativa were included in the Pharmacopoeias and Materia Medicas of allopaths and homeopaths alike in all the English-speaking countries; they were also included in the herbal lore of South America, Africa and Native American cultures:

> Many people may be unaware that herbal medicine served as the primary mode of medical practices in the United States until almost 1935. This practice did change as chemical medicine burst on the scene prior to 1935...for perhaps two thousand years, all plain physicians accepted and adhered to the...herbal...traditional systems. Yet this tremendous consensus among prominent medical authorities for two millennia is ignored. (Christi)

Nausea and lack of appetite are two of the primary uses for which Cannabis was recommended in the 19th century. From the Materia Medica by Ruddock - we learn: "Cannabis Sativa is cause for increasing the appetite, quelling the symptoms of nausea."

As a matter of fact, the medicinal uses for which Cannabis has been effective over the course of human evolution appear limitless. These age-old benefits can no longer be easily ignored since modern treatments often result in the need for increasingly larger and more lethal doses of drugs, culminating in loss of efficiency at best and horrendous, often non-reversible, problems in numerous cases. A second reason for the revival of more natural, less drastic remedies is the upsurge in information to a public eager to save the escalating cost of conventional medicine, especially with the realization that modern science often fails despite its technologies.

When it is poisoned, an organism automatically contracts. The cells are robbed of oxygen. The system becomes depressed. Even the workings of the brain are deranged. Marijuana Therapy acts to expand the entire body/mind by its autonomic investment, i.e., breathing becomes more efficient, allowing the cells to be re-oxygenated, thereby aiding in the elimination of the toxins. The dilation of blood vessels, the relaxation of the muscles, and the increased bifurcated fueling of the brain all work in symphonic harmony so that the entire system is rebalanced. The full extent of the action of marijuana on the organism is one of release of all tension - mental and physical - and easily translates into life affirming needs, such as the desire for food.

The fact that the results of the Life Sciences research with children was so favorable -"without any observable side effects" - leads us to realize that the occasional unpleasant side effects, reported in adult populations treated with Marijuana Therapy, are probably due to anxiety caused by internalized cultural brainwashing. It is to their credit that the authors of the Life Services article realized that, without prior prejudice, medical marijuana would probably not be accompanied by any unpleasantness at all: "We chose to administer delta-8-THC to children... (it) was the general (but not documented) belief that most side effects of delta-9-THC, in particular anxiety, are more prevalent in an adult population." This is probably also due to the loosening of the constrained breathing of adult populations not usual in youth.

As is usual in clinical treatment, before any drug is administered to human subjects, animal testing is done. In this case, monkeys, dogs, rats, and cats were given high doses of various isomers of cannabinoids. The data indicated effective anti-emetic properties as well as safety. The children were given delta-8-THC by mouth before the start of anti-cancer treatment - every six hours for 24 hours. In preliminary experiments on eight children, the clinicians stopped administering the cannabinoid after the first or second dose. "Vomiting stopped in most cases."

Therefore, in the actual test, the children were given four doses for a full 24 hours, which resulted in no vomiting whatsoever. This result was in keeping with those reported in modern research articles: "Cannabinoids are currently useful therapeutically to ameliorate the nausea and vomiting of cancer chemotherapy" (Borison).

Testing continues around the world with always favorable effects. Doctors can now follow their own patients in the legal states in the U.S. and have reported also favorable results. The truth has leaked out. Censorship and/or misinformation that exists in the mainstream media from book publishers to radio and TV talk shows, and includes the newspaper monopolies, and internet sites are being overwhelmed with the realization that the lay public is awakening. The medical world is becoming increasingly unable to ignore either the science or the interest of the patients. This is especially true among specialists, such as those in the field of cancer treatment.

In a random sample of over 1000 oncologists, in a survey taken to determine attitudes toward employing marijuana in treatment, revealed that more than half of those practicing physicians knew that marijuana worked in many cases where no conventional drug could. More to the point, nearly 25% of the oncologists surveyed were willing to admit that they had in the past recommended marijuana to their patients despite its illegality. These doctors for the most part represented the younger age groups, having graduated medical school in the late 60s, 70s, 80s and

90s. "Of the respondents who expressed an opinion, a majority thought marijuana should be available – but by prescription." According to Dr. Silverberg (from the Life Sciences study), "there has evolved an unwritten but accepted standard of treatment within the oncologic community which readily accepts marijuana's use."

> Oncologists may prefer to prescribe smoked marijuana over oral THC for several reasons. The bio-availability of THC absorbed through the lungs has been shown to be more reliable than that of THC absorbed through the gastrointestinal tract, smoking (and now vaporization) offers patients the opportunity to self-titrate dosages to realize therapeutic levels with a minimum of side effects, and there are active agents in the crude marijuana that are absent from the pure synthetic THC.

An old and misplaced study from the 70s from the New Mexico State Department reported on 169 volunteers: (1) efficacy of marijuana to reduce the nausea and vomiting associated with chemotherapy when conventional medicines had failed; and (2) the superiority of smoked marijuana vs. the ingestion of the synthetic THC pill (Marinol) in reducing vomiting to a statistically significant degree. Prior familiarity did not lessen the effectiveness of Marijuana Therapy. i.e., no tolerance to marijuana existed from the point of view of medical efficaciousness; and the feeling of being high was also not a factor, i.e., some patients just stopped vomiting but reported no change in consciousness. Owing to diligent searching for this study, this misplaced document was located and made public.

Glaucoma

"Glaucoma is in many ways a mysterious disease process. It is more than merely the reflection of IOP or a fluid deficit or a change in the optic nerve head." -- Keith Green

Through the investigation necessary to write this article, it was found that vast number of sentient beings - cats, dogs, mice, geese, rabbits and monkeys ~ are/were tortured and killed for the sake of progress. As early as the 70s, the medical profession knew full well that smoking marijuana could be a significant remedy for glaucoma. It was at that time that the "Compassionate Use Program" was first instituted by the Federal Government (that supplied and continues to supply 300 marijuana cigarettes a month to a few selected individuals – one of whom has Glaucoma.) Cannabis causes a dramatic decrease in pressure within the chambers of the eye, a pressure that, otherwise, all too often results in blindness. Many tests were launched to discover the exact mechanics of how each unique cannabinoid worked, so that their "mystery" could be understood and the essential healing substance within the marijuana plant could be synthesized and controlled (in a pill by prescription). The eyes of thousands of animals were drugged and dissected in scientific laboratories and the experimental results were reported in detail in a zealous attempt to reduce the synergistic psychobiological process of "seeing" and its interface with marijuana to the least common denominator.

Underlying these reductionistic methods is a philosophy that considers human beings superior to and independent from the total creation. Conventional medicine manipulates the surroundings to accommodate this illusion of separation and strives to suppress the symptoms of an unbalanced philosophy and way of life. There is little concern of future manifestations of a yet greater disequilibrium, except in the laboratories where animals are sacrificed in the search to synthesize new drugs.

Holistic healing strives to reverse the causes of instability in the physical and emotional life, helping a patient connect with the environment, thereby harmonizing the whole person. Ironically, despite all the vivisection (or as I'd like to think, because of it), marijuana's beneficial effect on glaucoma has remained mysterious.

The verb "to see" describes an extremely sophisticated process by which we sense or detect the outer world through a complicated interpretation of radiant energy in the frequency of visible light. "To see" also connotes mental cognition which stems from the anatomical fact that the organ of sight is the most evolved - and the most recently evolved-outgrowth of the human brain. The optic nerve (which sees) is an "outpouching" from the forebrain and is identical in tissue composition to the brain. This sensitive and incredibly sophisticated extension of the "seat of the intellect" travels toward the exterior surface of the body to sense or "see" the outer surrounding and to relay the data back to the brain for interpretation. We should note that 40% of all sensory input to the brain comes from our eyes.

For such a complicated and fragile process as sight to succeed: the medium through which it operates, the appendages by which it is protected, and the system from which it is nourished and cleansed must all function in intricate interdependence. This happens within an unimaginably tiny area, made of minute capillaries of nourishment and microscopic cavernous channels of drainage which are all in profound and constant communication with each other, always invested with direction from the brain's interpretation of what is needed at any given moment.

Aqueous Humor: The Medium of Nourishment

The eyeball is filled with a clear, watery fluid called the Aqueous Humor and separated into two main compartments, the Anterior Chamber, a small elliptical slit between the iris and the cornea, and the Posterior Chamber, which makes up the remaining portion. The Aqueous fluid, which is electromagnetically charged to transmit light, is in constant flux, being produced in the Posterior Chamber in the "ciliary process," flowing into the Anterior Chamber and then draining into the "trabecular meshwork" (channels of drainage). Constancy of pressure, as well as the appropriate metabolic composition for nourishment and cleansing of surrounding tissues are maintained by a dynamic tension in the Aqueous Humor, which serves also as a protective envelope for the fragile optic nerve-head. The integrity of the shape of the eyeball is further sustained by the Aqueous.

In glaucoma, the eyeball (in all its functions) degenerates when the intraocular pressure (IOP) rises beyond the limits of tolerance for the optic nerve, causing irreversible damage and blindness. Ultimately, glaucoma is a failure of the brain's attempt to sense the outer world and make sense of it.

In the philosophy of holistic healing, all disease is rooted in functional cause. We may speculate that the brain, in its interpretation of what it sees, is "distressed," and that stress is reflected in the IOP rise or tension within the eyeball. This fits well with another speculation that the optic nerve-head itself may be undernourished, thereby causing the problem.

The Glaucomatous Process

An increase in Intraocular Pressure (IOP) beyond safe limits, sometimes suddenly, but usually gradually, with progressive vision failure; defines glaucoma. The rise in intraocular tension is related to an imbalance between the production of aqueous fluid and its drainage through normal exit channels. Production of the Humor is continuous and is refurbished completely every one to two hours. Drainage is likewise continuous and in the healthy eye; the drainage out should equal the inflow. The medical consensus is that obstruction exists inside and at the beginning of the drainage channels. Whether the imbalance is explained as too much fluid, or too little drainage, the end result is irreversible blindness unless remedied.

The Marijuana Remedy

Within about one hour after smoking marijuana, and for the four to five hours following, the IOP within the eyeball is dramatically reduced to safe limits even in the extremely high pressure associated with the latter stages of glaucoma. The drainage routes dilate and the reduced tension is reflected within the ciliary body which results in less call for aqueous formation. By Parasympathetic innervation, the outflow channels are relaxed and dilated. "There is an increased ...permeability," according to Dr. Keith Green. By increased Parasympathetic action, the inflow channels are constricted: "Vasoconstriction of the afferent feeder vessels of the ciliary body causes a pressure fall in the capillaries." Dr. Green continues: "This effect occurs concurrently and paradoxically by a mechanism which is not yet understood."

Because marijuana "sedates and stimulates" (as it was described over 100 years ago in the Indian Hemp Drugs Commission Report), it has a balancing effect on the Automatic Nervous System (ANS) that is unique and actually unstudied in Western medicine. This "balancing" effect has caused major confusion regarding how marijuana benefits so many stress-related diseases, in general, and glaucoma in particular. Confusion has resulted in untold experiments aimed at understanding the one way that Marijuana Therapy alleviates the IOP increases associated with glaucoma.

But Marijuana Therapy works in two ways - on both sides of the ANS - as no other known substance does (i.e. "paradoxically!"). Until this is "seen" in the cognitive sense (which is very difficult in the current medical framework of Either/Or drugs, instead of Both/And), and its importance understood, the working of Marijuana Therapy will remain an enigma.

First, the "miosis" (pupil constriction) effect of marijuana through the Parasympathetic side of the ANS causes less straining "to see," signifying a relaxed organ of sight compared to "End Stage Glaucoma," when (no hope is left) the pupil is as dilated as possible in a futile attempt to impact a degenerated optic nerve.

Second, the drainage of aqueous is integrated into the sinus drainage areas where the mucus is thinner and more motile owing to the effect of marijuana. Studies also show an increase of protein content of the humor with marijuana use, suggesting less need for more fluid as well as an increase of sodium transport because of increased tissue permeability.

Actually, glaucoma is a problem of increased blood pressure within the eye. Marijuana has been shown to lower blood pressure within the whole body, including the eye. We should again be reminded:

As it is not proper to try to cure the eyes without the head, nor the head without the body, so neither is it proper to cure the body without the soul, and this is the reason why so many diseases escape physicians who are ignorant of the whole. (Plato)

Experiments with Marijuana

Sadly, vivisection of countless animals is the norm. In one experiment, the autonomic nerves that travel to the eye were severed "ganglionectomized," in hundreds of animals. THC, extracted from the natural marijuana plant, was shown to lower the pressure in their eyeballs, even though the animals were alive and awake with their heads clamped in a vise! Of course, the THC didn't work nearly as well as before the maiming, when the local autonomic nerves were in place, but the decrease in IOP was still significant. The results of the study were also confusing since it was unclear how THC injected into the body affected the IOP when the local autonomic optic nerves were cut off. The researchers also discovered that nothing happened when THC was injected directly into the brain.

Marijuana Therapy provides more oxygenated blood to the brain and therefore to the optic nerve. We see better, and think better because we are not constricted – mentally or physically. From the objective scientist's understanding, the optic nerve is in need of nourishment, cleansing, and protection. "The notion that ocular damage depends on an imbalance of intraocular pressure and blood supply to the optic nerve...shifts the emphasis from IOP to the anatomic and physiologic

state of the optic nerve."
There is no consideration of any psychological component of "seeing" and its connection to glaucoma. Dissection of the physical components, instead of seeing into the whole is the thread that runs throughout the philosophy of today's science. Unfortunately, the scientific thought that dissects helpless animals, also dissect and extracts individual compounds from the marijuana plant that "show promise" as potential synthetic pharmaceuticals, notably: cannabinoid, cannabidiol, cannabinoic acid, cannabigerol, cannabicicyclol, and the isomers of Delta 1, 8 & 9. The entire point of the wholesome delivery of nature's herbal tonic is therefore circumvented; and the results of each specific extract have either less beneficial effect than the intact plant or no beneficial effect at all. "Awareness that marijuana lowered IOP has spurned a great effort to identify the mechanism by which this effect occurs, and (provide a) delivery system to the eye which can lower IOP without the well-known psychotropic side effects."

The Holistic Understanding

Mind (as the finest instrument of human processing) operates through the mechanical processes of the brain and "goes out" to experience, see, and interpret the surroundings. The natural propensity and main function of the brain is to serve as a vehicle by which the individual consciousness can realize (by its relationship with the world) itself. In this understanding, the optic nerve is the organ whereby nearly half of all data is detected to be deciphered and interpreted by the mind through the brain. The task of protection, nourishment, and cleansing are relegated to the automatic processes of balance, allowing for the higher centers to focus on more complex decisions.

In the ancient science of the Medicine of India (Ayurveda) organs degenerate because of overuse, under-use, or misuse. In glaucoma, whatever is interpreted by the brain as not-beneficial causes the ANS to respond - creating tension in the face of a perceived threat. This is an unconscious process that defines a personality type. If this reaction is long-standing, without relief, and if there is the corresponding constitutional weakness at that particular location, the organ degenerates.

No doubt, glaucoma has psychological underpinnings and that outward intervention is needed to facilitate the chronically non-relaxed person (organ). Marijuana Therapy serves the subtle parameters for relief of the complicated symptoms of glaucoma by potentially exposing the root of tension and eliminating its damaging expression. "Analysis suggests an indirect effect ...associated with relaxation." (Flom)

Discussion

Just because Marijuana Therapy can work so effectively, so safely and so economically, there is no definite reason for employing it, if pharmaceutical medicines were as good or better. The original reason marijuana lost favor was because its results were considered too variable, and our modern medical science demanded predictability:

> Pharmaceutical treatments are predictable all right:...after many years of research, NONE of them work as safely or as effectively as Marijuana Therapy, nor are they as easy to self-medicate in appropriate dosage. (Grinspoon)

Furthermore, in glaucoma research, Dr. Green reports that for marijuana use: "studies indicate that the IOP fall is as good as or better than most agents."

The fact that no control is necessary (because there is no danger of an overdose) and that individual patient control of dosage is better than the objective determination of a physician, represents the problem that Marijuana Therapy poses to the authority of the doctor, in contrast to the autonomy and sense of self-determination it affords the patient.

Marijuana Therapy is constant in its complete harmlessness and its absolute healthfulness. It has no deleterious side effects that researches can identify except the psychological component of feeling "high," which is mistakenly deemed a negative.

In some studies of marijuana, there was a lowering of blood pressure in the whole body upon first-time use that was uncomfortable, called "postural hypotension," where the patient needed to lie down for a few minutes to alleviate the feeling of faintness. Perhaps this extreme hypotension (which was momentary and only occurred upon the first-time experience) was caused by the fear that accompanies "seeing" things as they really are and perhaps being uncomfortable with the loss of defense mechanisms.

Other adverse effects noted are anxiety (which, of course, is related to the fear of psychological nakedness), as well as the increased energy that is unfamiliar; feeling hungry and thirsty (the munchies); and experiencing an increased heart rate. Another plus for Marijuana Therapy as opposed to conventional drugs is that there is no tolerance (as in the drug use). A single marijuana cigarette worked effectively, even when more had previously been used. This supports the "less is more" theory, a brilliant technical explanation given by John Gettman, in Marijuana & the Brain, Part II: The Tolerance Factor.

The approved conventional drugs for glaucoma are all dangerous to overall health, are fraught with horrendous side effects, and must be monitored continuously for life-threatening dangers. They are, however, completely controllable by the doctor, and precise doses of drugs are predictably available by prescription from the pharmaceutical giants at great cost to the patient.

The side effects of the conventional medicines, in contrast to the benign or beneficial aspects of marijuana, are numerous. Furthermore, as the treatment proceeds over time, synthetic medicines must be constantly altered. In fact, the longer one takes these "medicines," the more necessary it becomes to either increase dosage or switch to ever more dangerous drugs.

Some of the most noteworthy and common side effects of approved medical treatment for glaucoma include: headaches, drug allergy, metabolic acidosis, rashes, cataracts, hypotension, blood dyscrasia, kidney stones, and ulcers. When the synthetic pharmaceutical medicines fail – as they all do over time, owing to their one sidedness which assures tolerance -more aggressive medicines are employed whose side effects include hallucinations, anxiety, mania, bone marrow depletion, retinal detachment, cardiovascular bradycardia, and, finally, death from respiratory failure.

When all else fails and blindness is imminent, surgical opening of the outflow channels is attempted. The success rate is dismal. With the increased recognition of legal medical marijuana, in countries throughout the modern world, cannabis-based medicines are being designed for fast and easy access for the asthmatic patient (and others in need of the same immediacy). The last attempt at marketing the intact plant as a pharmaceutical remedy *needing a prescription* is a "spritz" bottle with juiced extract.

Multiple Sclerosis

We tend to believe that the ban on testing marijuana has resulted in a lack of documentation of its effects. But such is not the case. In the scientific literature, there exist thousands of studies that have investigated distinct elements of Cannabis in relationship to human physiology. These "cannabinoids" have been analyzed extensively in order to learn the secret mechanism of how they affect (the artificially separated components of) our constitutions. Each part of the puzzle of human reactivity to different Cannabis compounds stands alone and, so far, there is no acknowledgment of what these isolated discoveries suggest for the case of Marijuana Therapy.

In modern science, the only acceptable method for testing a drug is the "double-blind" investigation which assures objective determination of how a substance impacts on an organism at that time and place. Only the pharmaceutical companies are allowed to perform double-blind studies with marijuana because it is classified as a Schedule I Drug (the most dangerous type, without recognized medical value). The sinister agreement with the government was that only the pharmaceutical industry would be allowed to test marijuana for a 10-year period, during which time a synthetic would be developed that would fulfill the recognized medical promise of Cannabis without the psychoactive properties. Needless to say, this effort has not succeeded; neither has the ban been lifted to allow for the double-blind testing that science accepts as valid as was promised. Nevertheless, in the last few decades, studies in other countries have documented a wealth of general benefits and scientific indications for Marijuana Therapy.

In direct contrast to objective science, the ancient disciplines not only made note of the obvious effects of a remedy, but also amassed detailed descriptions of each patient's subjective experience. Since conscious regulation of one's own state of health was a sacred responsibility, primary respect was given to experiential assessment. Holistic medicine is the modern equivalent of this philosophy which encourages awareness of one's own body/mind in relationship to its surroundings.

Since the double-blind study is the only acceptable form of testing a medicine's efficiency, the medical community has itself become blind to the validity of individual testimony, even when vast numbers of individuals report similar benefits.

In hearings before the State of California to determine whether or not Marijuana Therapy ameliorated the symptoms of MS, the patients were sworn to tell the truth, and really had no reason whatsoever to lie, yet their "anecdotal" testimony was disregarded by the conventional health care professionals as being unscientific and therefore without value"

> Valerie Leith Cover: "Prior to smoking, I was throwing up and suffering from spasms. However, within five minutes of smoking marijuana, I stopped vomiting, no longer felt nauseous, and noticed my intense spasms were significantly reduced. The sense of "shakiness" which I constantly felt deep inside me seemed to diminish. At one point, without thinking, I stood up unaided!

Having been on a very high regimen of ACTH (which triggers the body to release mega-doses of its own steroids), and owing to severe and dangerous side effects, Mr. Paufler, another MS patient, decided – *for the third time* – to stop using this medication.

> Gary Paufler: "The ACTH was making me worse and the side effects were overwhelming me. I was bedridden. If it were a choice between the treatment and the disease, I would rather have MS. I was placed on prednisone (a steroid) in its place. Medical records indicate I died that day...there was a nearly total absence of potassium in my body from the prescribed drugs. I stopped all steroid drugs but continued using valium.
>
> "I began smoking marijuana...to get high. One evening some old friends came to visit, and we smoked several joints. When my friends got up to say good-bye, I stood up. Everybody stared. I was stunned. (Then) I walked. The longer I smoked marijuana, the better I got. My eyesight returned. I began walking, my spasms were nonexistent."

There are many more affidavits of patients who testified at those hearings, all equally dramatic, pointing to the untold benefits of Marijuana Therapy. The reactions of the medical profession in 1987:

> Dr. Donald H. Silverberg: "I have reviewed the affidavits...None are supported by scientific or medical findings...their claimed results.... are useless....Further, the negative effects of using marijuana...make it unacceptable for treating MS. Second...I know of no drug...used as in smoking form. Also....The use of (marijuana) especially for long term treatment would be worse than the original disease itself."
>
> Dr. Kenneth P. Johnson: "The information regarding the use of marijuana...is purely anecdotal....I must conclude that marijuana should remain in Schedule 1 (because) I cannot conclude that marijuana is effective in treating M.S."

But since 1987, Marijuana Therapy has been proven over and over again in rigorous scientific studies to: 1) diminish even sometimes eliminate the symptom, and 2) stop the progression of the disease and possibly to reverse the damage to the myelin.

Since MS is a disease that is treated mainly for its symptoms, the doctors have tried just about anything imaginable that might help this energetic failing - from electrical current, to diet, to vitamin therapy – in hope of spurring repair of damaged nerve fibers, they have used all range of depressants to dampen the spasticity associated with MS, and recently, the employment of immune suppressants to slow, or try to eliminate yet further deterioration to the nerve bundles.

The majority of conventional medicines are so concentrated as to affect the organism immediately and aggressively in hope of suppressing the symptoms of discomfort. Pharmaceutical treatment is employed nearly across the board, even though every study readily acknowledges that the intricate physical-chemical mechanisms that these concentrated drugs trigger is not understood: "studies of short term therapy with brief periods of follow-up consistently demonstrate that corticosteroids, particularly in large doses, can alter almost any aspect of the immune system. There are no studies yet on long term hazards."

The short term dangers of the corticosteroids that are known include: malignancy, irreversible reductions in immune response balance, hypertension, diabetes, anemia, renal insufficiency, venous thrombosis, herpes zoster infection, urosepsis, flu, depression, rash, blood toxicity, loss of strength, hallucination, tremor, ulcers, meningitis, hypotension, ataxia, drowsiness, heart disturbance, bone marrow suppression, seizures.

The approximate cost of Betaseron, a popular aggressive medication given to MS patients, exceeds $10,000 per year. Total profit to its pharmaceutical manufacturer would be $645 million per year, if we assume use by 150,000 of the 250,000 MS patients in the U.S.

On the other side, far away from the crowd of commercialized concentrations, is Cannabis. This plant of exquisite beauty and incredible strength, of ubiquitous adaptation, and of primordial connection on a cellular level with life on this planet, has been the subject of great interest and intensive study over the past several decades. Its most well-known physical effects seem especially tailored to the needs of MS patients. Sometimes, with Marijuana Therapy nearly miraculous abatement of the weakness, spasticity, and mental depression associated with Multiple Sclerosis has been demonstrated and is documented in the scientific literature. Buried in the research of the past 30 years are 2018 experiments with marijuana and/or its various compounds that demonstrate the scientific reasons as to HOW marijuana works to restore balance and integrate coordination m patients who are in dire need of medical help and mental hope.

The THC molecule impacts the cannabinoid receptors throughout the Autonomic Nervous System which directs our involuntary body/mind reactions. Immediately upon smoking marijuana, we breathe more fully and our breath is more fully oxygenated. The severe weakness associated with MS is just as immediately lessened. More oxygen is delivered to the entire body - including to the atrophied oxygen deprived muscles -which in time feel stronger (because they are). The brain is likewise delivered more oxygen and, since THC provides a bilateral, balanced delivery to this bifurcated organ, this helps lessen symptoms of spasms and vertigo.

As early as 1992, a study was reported in the Medical Journal of Australia that found: "in experienced smokers, marijuana smoking was accompanied by a significant bilateral increase in cerebral blood flow," and further on. "Marijuana is known to increase sensory awareness which may account for the increase in blood flow after marijuana use" (Caswell).

Of course, this logic is not in order. We know that enhancement of sensory awareness is a result, not a cause, of the increased blood flow to the brain. Nevertheless, this study was done according to double-blind rules and therefore proved by deduction what we already knew. More to the point, specifically in reference to MS, which has as one of its direct problems a loss of circulation in the brain capillaries, we now have proof that marijuana reverses this symptom.

"Tough physical training to improve the circulation in. the capillaries of the CNS" would be helpful for the patient." (Russell) But without any tough physical training, which is a ludicrous notion for an incapacitated victim of MS, who may not be able to walk, talk, or even see, Marijuana Therapy unquestionably accomplishes this needed increase in capillary circulation.

Loss of coordination (ataxia) a very common occurrence in MS; it is one of the main debilitations reported to be dramatically improved with Marijuana Therapy. A study conducted by the Federal Republic of Germany demonstrated that smoking marijuana "may have powerful beneficial effects on both spasticity and ataxia."

The drugs that are usually administered for MS almost invariably help one symptom while aggravating another. The drugs that decrease spasticity are depressants which, as a side effect, further the symptoms of weakness and loss of coordination. And they also have the dangerous side effects (already listed) common to one-sided drugs. Spasticity is an excessive activity of motor neurons and an associated lack of reciprocal energizing. Scientific studies discovered one of the secrets of Marijuana Therapy when they found that both THC and CBD (another Cannabis compound) caused:

increased firing threshold in individual neurons. Maybe cannabinoids modulate the intra-cellular metabolism and regulate the activity of multiple cellular processes.

Actually, because of the way THC affects the entire physiology (slightly increased heart rate and increased capacity of the lungs), the damaged, oxygen-deprived nerves are reinvigorated or upgraded in their capacity - if not to normal, then at least to "better than – before." The muscle spasticity is generally relieved, owing to the relaxation of the entire musculature.

People with MS often lose sensation in their extremities. When the nerves are more fully fueled, as happens with Marijuana Therapy, this discomfort diminishes. Laboratory testing of THC demonstrated increased sensory awareness, which validates what marijuana, smokers have always known.

THC, however, is also defined and maligned as "psychoactive," which simply means (in functional terminology) that a person's outlook becomes fuller, broader, and more energized. We know that marijuana balances our involuntary physiology. This includes the mental depression that results from a downtrodden and narrow perspective of one's own personal situation. The "Lifting of the Spirit", that accompanies Marijuana Therapy is in perfect keeping with its scientific laboratory findings, on a cellular level - of more sensations - including clearer insight of one's predicament.

The diagnosis of MS follows a series of complicated tests which show damage to the insulation surrounding nerve fibers in the brain and in the spinal cord. Conventional treatment attempts to halt further damage by administering aggressive medications (corticosteroids) that suppress the over-active immune system which has gone askew and is thereby causing, or at least allowing, the damage. Conventional medicine is actually trying to rebalance or "modulate" this over-excited immune system.

Of course, working unilaterally and aggressively on one side of any bifurcated organic system will result in an equal rebound action, which is the reason immuno-suppressants are so dangerous. No synthetic drug has yet been manufactured that has "immune modulating" effects; instead, drugs act in an either exciting or depressing fashion. The miracle of THC in its effect on the immune system, however, has now been found to be "immuno modulating" (Kusher). This is a significant discovery and one which suggests that marijuana is not indicated just for the symptoms of MS, but may actually help to halt its usual progression.

But marijuana imparts much more than just the effects of the famous THC molecule. It is comprised of hundreds of unique cannabinoids which scientists have shown match or "fit" receptors in our DNA. There is a receptor for CX5 (another cannabinoid) which suggests "highly conserved throughout human-evolution" profile. In other words, CX5 was an evolving companion to human evolution.

According to a study in Great Britain, "CX5 suggests a possible role in inflammatory and immune responses (because) its human receptor is on a macrophagic cell," which cells are thought to play an "immuno-modulating role."

The anti-inflammatory, immuno-modulating sophistication of just one cannabinoid (among hundreds) as demonstrated by the scientific community's own tests is available for all to see in university libraries in every city in the country. The increased blood flow in the brain with its resultant increase in sensibility, coordination, sense of balance, and overall strengthening, is well documented in pharmaceutical studies. There is no scientific basis for accusing patients of not knowing what they mean when they detect a "sense of well being," but Dr. Kenneth Johnson did just that: "It is difficult to determine what the patient claims marijuana did – especially the claim that it improved 'sense of well-being'…it is virtually impossible for any drug to cause the miraculous and immediate improvements claimed by the patient."

All these chemical dissections of marijuana in the laboratory point to balancing and modulating benefits. However, as we travel through these reductionistic experiments, the importance of the intact Cannabis plant's interdependent molecular effects must never be forgotten. The beneficial indications of each isolated compound of Cannabis are just modest whispers of what the whole and holy ancient Sativa promises. Yet, although in some progressive locations where the laws are now allowing Marijuana Therapy as an effective treatment for MS, still many, many seriously sick people are being denied the best medicine available, because too many doctors believe suffering from MS (or any disease) is preferable to using the herbal medicine that provides relief.

According to Grinspoon, patients report that they find smoked herbal Cannabis better at controlling their symptoms than synthetic derivatives, and "Cannabis may even retard the progression of the disease"

Questions/Answers/Commentary

In the course of distributing preliminary copies of this book to various reviewers, Jon Hanna presented some questions that deserve in-depth answers, because they are questions on everyone's mind.

J.H. - "Wouldn't it be hard for a regular user of marijuana who was used to its balancing effect on the ANS to go back to the "stressful" ups and downs of a normally functioning body? Couldn't there be withdrawal symptoms associated with this? I know that my brother-in-law (a habitual, chronic marijuana smoker) who is normally an extremely easy going guy turns very cranky when he is out of pot for a few days. And Terrence McKenna (a habitual pot smoker) relates what happened when he quit smoking pot: "... so then I did quit for two months, and what I did notice was a tremendous narrowing of my consciousness." Can a person be addicted to "higher consciousness?"

Answer - Stressful ups and downs are difficult for everyone. Stress is the reason for the unhealthy yet acceptable habits of smoking tobacco, using sugar, drinking alcohol, watching TV. If a person has found a healthy way of warding off stress, and the healthy way is then no longer available to him/her, such as jogging each day, meditating regularly, eating healthful foods, or using marijuana on a daily basis, there is no doubt that the person will feel unbalanced, cranky and normally stressed.

The issue of consciousness must be seen from a slightly different perspective. Addiction is a reaction to imbalance, which leads to none other than continued and more skewed imbalance. Consciousness is born of balance, and once the organism is out of sync, by definition, higher consciousness disappears. In order for someone who usually maintains balance through marijuana (and enjoys the attendant higher awareness born of that balance) to continue in a higher state of consciousness without marijuana, another stabilizer would be needed. Balance restored through work on oneself, such as meditation, prayer, yoga, breathing exercises, cognitive conversion, results in a raised consciousness. The practice of marijuana is not different than any other. As a student of yoga, one must constantly do his/her discipline, so must the Christian priest or nun practice prayer and partake of the sacraments as a constant lifelong discipline. In all spiritual endeavors, it is hoped that regular and continuous practice will so habituate the aspirant in warding off programs of self-serving desires, that he/she will be graced with a permanent equanimity. Any transgression from the ideal is but a sign post that the practitioner must keep on working.

Jon also questioned my assessment that the "short term memory loss" associated with marijuana is a "marijuana myth." I hope I can clear up this confusion.

If you're riding in a car at 60 miles an hour, looking out the window at the scenery of mountains and trees, the attention you can pay to any one tree is very superficial. The perception you are having is through a very large "window of consciousness" (Fishkin & Jones) with a tremendous amount of stimulation being admitted, whose rate of movement is quite fast (Sympathetic Mode / Stimulation), When the car is nearly at a stand still, only one tree may be in what has now become a much smaller "window of consciousness." It will appear in greater depth because you will be taking in details not before available to your quickly moving, although larger window (Parasympathetic Mode / Relaxation).

Marijuana BOTH enlarges the window by giving a perspective that can sometimes be termed "global" AND slows down the rate of "attentional shift" (Fishkin and Jones) to a concentrated mode of intensity, sometimes to where it appears as though "time stands still." We can also understand this experience, psychologically, as the state where there is no ego or awareness of separate orchestration between oneself and the universe. It can be a magnetic experience because of its intensity.

When we deepen our intensity of attention (because we've slowed down and have time and energy to use for intensification of awareness) and also widen our window of consciousness, according to this model, a "receptive mode" (neither active nor passive) is entered. In yogic science, we are said to become more "aware" and "one -pointed" in our depth of understanding the underlying reality. Life, in general feels less random, has meaning, and is interesting. These features define an altered state of consciousness (Tart) only because it is unusual to our usual way of being. (In this understanding of altered states of consciousness, less interest is paid to the common trivia of mundane existence. If we become accustomed to this sharpness of perception, as with regular marijuana use or various techniques to increase our mindfulness or consciousness, the altered state nomenclature is no longer as valid nor is the intensification of awareness as magnetic. That is why - when we use marijuana regularly -we tend to feel as though we no longer "get high." Getting high assumes raising up from a lower, less full experience, and the act of raising up itself represents the altering which is sought as an event that gives a shock and thereby helps us to notice the underlying reality - which is a natural, innate, although suppressed, human need, neither recognized nor fulfilled, for the most part, in or by modern society. Instead daily life is not really all that momentous because we don't take time, have time, or even know that we need time. The overly active mode of taking in all manner of information at a very fast pace is the short-term memory "skill" necessarily encouraged in modern life. It is neither healthy nor natural for our organism, but it is the way to function most successfully on the treadmill of contemporary life. It is the skewed-toward-Sympathetic overload, about which this entire book was written.

When one is paying very close attention to the meaning/beauty/ function of some things, less energy or interest is available to other things, especially things without such import, which is what often happens in the *marijuana experience* during times where we just don't pay close attention to, for example, a conversation. This is the short-term memory disassociation from the activity around us that can happen with marijuana. But to call it a "loss" is inappropriate because:

1. When one learns anything or notices anything while having the *marijuana experience*, the memory of it, as well as the present experience, is greater/keener and fuller and also easier to retrieve and less lost over time. According to Fishkin and Jones, "should memory be sampled under the influence of marijuana, It could be done with greater intensity and with a greater flow of deeper-lying or unusual associations being brought into consciousness."

2. "Loss" implies having the information, as a permanent registration in the mind -which doesn't happen with marijuana "disassociation", instead there is no registration of the event to the memory bank. The deposit is never made. Only when a deposit in the bank is made will the memory of it be clearer and easier to retrieve if made while experiencing marijuana.

3. "Short-term memory loss" smacks of senility not at all like the

marijuana experience. Senility/Alzheimer's Disease becomes increasingly worse over time because the window of consciousness is foggy, stuck at one point of reference, and the link between it (the window) and the long term memory storage area shorts out or becomes clogged to access - all of which can be translated into the hardening of the arteries of the brain found in autopsy reports of Alzheimer patients, even in young victims.

This memory loss includes not knowing one's relatives, how to dress, or what is socially acceptable. The person actually "forgets" or loses something he/she had at a previous time. With marijuana, the present perception and the long-term memory bank are more in communication NOT less, because of the greater blood flow to all areas and nerves of the brain, and also because non-verbal comprehension increase (Fishkill and Jones) - which allows for the experience to be fuller or more. The meaning is clearer. "Nonverbal" corresponds to the intensification of flash understandings or intuitions. Interest in the now naturally leads away from inconsequential events and therefore can rightly be termed as a "loss of interest" of any particular occurrence. Important issues are not disregarded because marijuana affects the person in a way that enhances awareness of important issues as well as increasing the desire to be more conscientious in issues of import.

4. The "loss of interest" to certain indoctrinated activities (which may create lapses in attention to mundane things), while disturbing to the onlooker, is overcome simply by intentional refocusing on the subject by the person in an altered state or higher consciousness.

A common experience for marijuana users (is) to say they can come down at will, that if they find themselves in a situation they feel unable to cope with adequately while in the altered state of consciousness of marijuana...(they) can deliberately suppress...effects. (Sugarman and Tarter)

Disinterest (not loss of memory or noticing), immediately evaporates during an emergency completely unlike brain dysfunction as in Alzheimer's Disease. Remember: the balance of marijuana is quite natural to the healthy organism. When an emergency presents, the Sympathetic mode is instantaneous. From balance, the appropriate response is easily accomplished. We can liken the "disassociation" from immediate trivia that occurs with the experiences of marijuana as something similar to the absent-minded-professor stereotype -, without suggesting that all experiences of marijuana is Einstein-like. Thousands of years ago, the Chinese prescribed Cannabis to increase and maintain one's memory; so they knew then what we are just beginning to understand.

5. and, probably most important, this effect of "disassociation of interest" is immediately reversible upon discontinuance of marijuana. We can also note that, as the high state becomes more familiar, less disassociation will occur since the novelty of that experience is no longer quite as magnetic.

6. Finally, fear of this disinterest to cultural values (of extreme competitiveness) scares the mainstream. This is because of a total lack of comprehension of the naturalness of being "high" and its healthfulness for the citizenry and future on the planet.

The misgivings concerning marijuana as a beneficial agent, unfortunately, are still very much a part of the mainstream mentality. The answers to those misgivings remain the same. However, what has changed completely is that educated guesses about how marijuana is so very beneficial to the human race, along with the deductive reasoning of holistic practice, and the empirical understanding of millions of people world-wide are now all backed up with scientific reality. There is no longer any question as to whether or not marijuana is harmful to our memories or to our brains. Hundreds of studies conducted over the last twenty years have enlightened the scientists and validated the *marijuana experience*. The benefits of marijuana for our brains and for our minds is now written in every language and accessible on every computer. The science of the Cannabinoid Network and how it nurtures our organisms is already being taught in institutions of higher learning. The truth is once again being rediscovered.

Chapter 6 • Politics of Prohibition
Confessions of a Drug Counselor

As a drug counselor within a country agency, I was constantly exposed to mainstream health-care jargon. "Self-Medicating" was the derogatory label reserved for clients' behavior, almost all of whom were attending Drug Counseling against their will as an alternative to prison. I was an imposter amidst the social work mentality that prevails within the hallowed walls of the Mental Health Community.

Friday was "case conference" day during which all the employees would gather together to ridicule a few previously designated clients. We would sit in a circle with our coffee, cigarettes, and candy, and discuss with smug superiority, the foolhardiness of all the "self-medicators." The staff was composed of the "boss," who was unabashedly addicted to valium; two "recovering" (sometimes) alcoholics; two incredibly obese social workers; a few young interns; and me. As an imposter in psychologist costume, whose heart was with all those people who were self-medicating their disease, it was infuriating to maintain my disguise. I ascribe to the unpopular, although well recognized, thought in Humanistic Psychology that therapy traverses a fragile line between mending the non-integrated personality and manipulating it to fit within the social norm. The message in today's society is to denigrate the notion of higher consciousness, despite the fact that all in-depth psychological studies recognize the value inherent in such an essential experience. Reminding my co-workers of this danger all too often set me apart from the agency's stated purpose - which was none other than to monitor and control the use of all illegal drugs by the client - and failing at that - to send the adjudicated customer directly to jail.

For the most part, the agency's clientele was under 30, and the crime was getting caught either using or selling herb. There were, of course, some who used hard drugs, whose lives were in constant upheaval. These cases were difficult. After a few years I realized there was a spiritual void which drove such destructive behavior. Only a super-effort of undistracted interest along with compassion, could touch these hard core addicts. My own suggestion - to substitute herb for heroin had to be couched in careful phrases lest the establishment get wind of my true identity.

Holistic Health counseling shares the philosophy of Systems Theory except that the system is perceived as far broader than the term usually denotes, taking into account not only behavior, motivation, and interaction with and from the outside world, but also dealing with the subjective, universal, and deep needs of human beings, which are always of a spiritual nature, however costumed, and including the influence that the counselor not only exerts on the client but also how the client-counselor experience impacts and enriches the world of both.

In the separatist world of professional psychology, the notion of becoming friends with one's clients is taboo for it blurs the lines between the authoritarian position and the subservient state of the un-empowered. When I worked within the boundaries of the County Agency, this rule of segregation was difficult to abide. Needless to say, I followed no such rigid formula in my own practice. "Counselor" is a "user friendly" term to replace the arrogant, dated, nomenclature of "therapist." Holistic Health, with its main focus on self-responsibility, goes one step further to a teacher/student model. I considered myself a teacher who imparted knowledge and encouragement, and many of my former students became my friends. Holistic counseling also recognizes that what is the best direction for the three dimensions of human life (body/mind/soul) may not be the most socially acceptable. In the case of two clients who were alcoholic outcasts, this was definitely true. To overcome the numbness of alcohol, I suggested to them (and to other clients) that they increase their regular marijuana ingestion. Additional use of marijuana proved to be very good medicine as well as a wonderful aid to concentrating the mind for study. My students, who had been inebriated for so long, began to awaken from their stupor.

If alcoholics can learn to take in progressively more pot and less booze, at some point the individual consciousness reasserts itself and the mechanical drive to be drunk, along with all its pitfalls, becomes a conscious, controllable desire instead of a self-propelling reaction.

The therapeutic 50-minute hour was often uplifting, despite the troubled life situations of my subjects. It was refreshing to share the mental set of these non-programmed "criminals" who dared to self-medicate themselves and their friends, and who were consequently policed by the state. Urine testing was mandatory, and supposed to be a surprise. It's interesting to note that urinalysis is only truly effective in detecting psychedelic plants, since all the hard (manufactured) drugs (including alcohol) are metabolized in a few days. The client need only stop "using" 48 hours before the counseling session for a "clean" result.

Also a doctor's prescription for methadone/thorazine/valium/prozac/etc. exempts the user from sanctions. During the three years that I worked at the agency, I administered many drug tests. Through some fortuitous circumstance for my clients, I was always able to drop some subtle hint to defuse the element of surprise. None of "my" clients ever tested positive. Nothing I did was ever responsible for sending anyone to prison.

That was over 20 years ago, when the drug war was in full swing. It is only now that I understand the medical profession's abhorrence of self-medication. I received my Holistic Health training under the umbrella of the ancient teaching of Indian philosophy. Self-regulation and assuming full responsibility for one's own ailments is actually the goal of life in all ancient spiritual philosophy. Yet, it is the antithesis of the Western Medical Model which fosters complete dependence on the doctor (and the pharmaceutical/insurance industry). Obviously, anything that smacks of autonomous wisdom threatens the power of the state. But, if we get permission by the doctor, pay the pharmacist, or even obtain our numbness at the hands of the bartender who collects the government's taxes - if we change our brain waves with sugar, deaden them with TV, computer games, videos - still we are not expanded in consciousness, and the threat of true sight does not loom. Only the psychedelics can terrorize the powers that be, for with them we are able to rebalance our psyches and neutralize our dis-ease. In addition, we can grow them, forage for them and pay no government taxes (or insurance premiums). To self-medicate ourselves, to be autonomous, to make choices, to grow in wisdom and not in status are the values that can eventually topple the established, short-sighted policies that choose profit before people.

A Letter from Jail
Joan Bello, POW

Dear Friends & Holy Smokers: It looks curiously like any sleep-away camp, but without clue as to the season, year or even the country. It's 2 AM, and the overhead fixtures have been turned off for the past 3 hours. Everyone is asleep in their bunks but me. Unusually bright night lights cast an eerie yellow outline of 22 single beds around the perimeter of a conspicuously barren room. There are no decorations on the walls, no night stands, no curtains on the eight plastic windows that obviously never open, and no clock, A few beds have pictures taped to headboards showing children and memories from different times.

The camp fantasy has quickly faded to the sinister reality. If I unhitch my usual thinking process - and let the emanation of this unnatural conglomerate of women impinge on my consciousness – I can actually feel an overwhelming and grossly inappropriate emotion of sheer indifference.

They say human beings will adjust to nearly any situation, accepting even the most uncomfortable conditions. The women here have surely done just that. They live in limbo, wondering when their time to rejoin life on the outside will come. Most of them are without financial resources, which automatically relegates them to sitting in jail – often for nearly a year – even though they have never been convicted of anything.

Once incarcerated, the injustice and inhumanity of the system becomes acutely obvious. Sanity is maintained by an assumed apathy and quiet resignation. But I am acutely aware that this outward display of acceptance is just a defense mechanism against the rage that seethes in the other women inmates - as I feel it too.

I understand for the first time what an unjust and cruel society we have conceived and why so many deprived people are driven to violence. I can taste the fear of having no freedom. I feel the fury of an unfamiliar anger which leads to images of revenge. But, miraculously, I am also experiencing all this from a distance.

I am in the meditative zone of being high. Here in jail, alone and remembering the sacred effect of the Marijuana Spirit, I am one with that vibration. I am in awe of the realization that over years and years of experience with being high by the grace of Holy Hemp that I have learned how to uncouple from the conditioning without benefit of the embodied Sativa. The Grace of the Spirit within the Cannabis plant has been imparted to me just by mentation!

Ironically, the magnificence of this hallowed experience is the reason why I am in jail, and why my husband sat in jail before me, not to mention the hundreds of thousands of peace-loving Americans who are presently incarcerated. Those of us who are the casualties in the front lines of the marijuana witch hunt are, of course, the best versed in all the depraved reasons our militaristic government is waging this criminal war on innocent citizens. Our numbers sadly keep growing as our commitment to the inalienable, natural right to medicate ourselves, pursue our own methods toward enjoyment, and worship the Divinity in the best way we can imagine grows ever stronger, gathering more and more people from all walks of life and all disciplines of science. Our prisons are inadequate to house what has become the most populated prison-society in the developed world because our laws define natural actions as crimes. The political system that upholds this foolhardy, cruel, unjustifiable policy is bolstered by the drive for profit.

The prison industry is booming, the police-state tactics are escalating, lawyers and judges are inundated with work. Meanwhile, the medical profession continues to close ranks around pharmaceutical synthetics even as the death toll in side effects reaches horrendous proportions. These foolhardy and extremely harmful activities are taking place in spite of the fact that one natural plant could end all the pain. The suffering of so many sick and dying people could be lifted, dangerously diminishing forests could be protected from constant exploitation, billions of hungry, unfortunate people around the globe could be given sustenance, the air itself could be cleaner and certainly the entire population could breathe better.

CANNABINOIDS

Substances that bind to Cannabinoid receptors of the Cannabinoid System in human and animal bodies.

There are Three Types of Cannabinoids:

1. Herbal – from the Cannabis Sativa Plant;
2. Endogenous – from bodies of humans and other animals;
3. Synthetic – from the laboratory

The Cannabinoid System has been around for over 600 million years! Before the dinosaurs! (Science discovered it only 10 years ago.)

Cannabinoids are in every living animal on the planet. (all animals naturally get high!)

The body is homeostatically maintained by the Cannabinoid System! (It balances the whole organism.)

Mother's milk has a booster shot of (endogenous) cannabinoids so the babies can learn to eat.   (Babies get the munchies naturally!)

Cannabinoids protect against sunburn and skin cancer because there are cannabinoid receptors all over the skin.

(Cannabis butter rubbed on the body gets the person high!)

Cannabinoids slow down the aging process. (High is Healthy)

Activity in the evolutionary advanced areas of the brain is increased in cannabinoid receptors and promotes higher consciousness.

(Greater comprehension is available to the higher and *smarter* levels.)

Cultures in Contrast

In keeping with the triple dimension of human experience, the battle to free marijuana is being waged on three fronts: recreational, medicinal, and sacramental. Essentially the secular argument is based upon a citizen's right to choose his/her form of enjoyment. Unlike alcohol, tobacco, caffeine, and even sugar - all proven to have devastating effects on our bodies - Cannabis consumption exhibits absolutely no harm either to the person or the society. In total contradiction to the shameless government-orchestrated propaganda, and in light of the myriad, in-depth tests attempting to discredit this magnificent· plant, no serious studies have documented any detriment stemming from enjoying the bounty of the hemp. In the medical marijuana arena, all the research shows that the close to 500 known molecular constituents of Cannabis are miraculously and undeniably beneficial for treating a wide range of diseases-from both dysfunctional psychic disturbances to physical derangements – and the list keeps growing! (See Testimony of Patients.) This is a list of all the patients who gave testimony as plaintiffs for The Class Action Lawsuit for Therapeutic Cannabis. Since that time, thousands of patients have given statements (concerning their medical use of marijuana and the help it affords them) before state legislatures, prestigious professional institutions, as well as to the newspapers, the judges, and the doctors. The Class Action Lawsuit Plaintiffs were the first group of patients to defy the unjust law and make their need public. Their statements are moving documentation of the astonishing extent to which Cannabis is needed for medicine.)

Examining the persecution we endure because of our recognition of marijuana as sacrament reveals the irreverence of our society. Organized religion bears little (if any) resemblance to glorifying the universally- felt life-giving force. Instead, the original kernel of spiritual revelation has degenerated into commercialized institutions interested in power and wealth, purposely stripped of all rituals and practices that might evoke the profound inner knowledge of the Divine. As a matter of fact, experiential knowledge of the sacred is actually feared by today's religious authorities:

> Many Churchmen (are) aligning themselves ... against the value of personal religious experience (because those who have spiritual

encounters) are inclined to follow their own inner direction rather than that of temporal authority. (Stafford and Golightly)

But, regardless of disparagement, persecution or prosecution inflicted by the power structure (secular or religious) upon those of us who have awakened to higher consciousness through the blessing of marijuana (or other sacred plants of wisdom), our faith is unshaken.

There is a central human experience which alters all other experiences...It is the center that gives understanding to the whole. Once found, life is altered forever because the very root of human identity has been deepened, (Van Dusen)

This is the realm of human life, beyond self-centeredness, which the Western infancy has yet to apprehend and which, in the wisdom of the East, has been systematically cultivated with the aid of marijuana for thousands of years.

Cannabis Sativa is regarded by the Hindus as a holy plant and the origin of this conception can be traced to the Vedic period...Yogis are well-known consumers of bhang...looked upon with some veneration...considered to possess super natural powers. (Merlin)

If we imagine that the efficiency of the human organism operates along a continuum ranging from severe sickness to optimum wellness, we will understand the Eastern coalescence of medicine with religion. Even the historical Jesus, as in the Biblical portrayal of a holy man, ministered to and miraculously cured the sick. In fact, ancient cultures around the world, so-called "primitive" societies that are still extant, combine their communion with the natural order with mystical knowledge of healing.

The East views optimum wellness as the ultimate state of alert calmness or "enlightenment," the goal of yoga, meditation, and devotional service. Marijuana, with its simultaneous sedative and stimulant effect, has been the constant companion of these spiritual disciplines for as long as their recorded history (over 5000 years ago).

Experientially speaking, marijuana "lifts the spirit" by evoking the trophotropic response:

...a response whose physiologic changes (are) similar to those measured during the practice of meditation... the trophotropic response (is) ... a protective mechanism against the over stress belonging to the trophotropic system and promoting restorative processes. (Hess)

It can be further defined as the state that exists owing to serotonin release by the brain - which specifically integrates the autonomic, psychic, and somatic functions of the human organism at a level below awareness but with measurable, physiologic interactions that are balanced in a dynamic antagonism by the opposing side of this dualistic interplay – known as the ergo-tropic response, understood as the central Parasympathetic arousal as it is mediated by serotonin. This physiological reaction (experienced subjectively as well-being) emanates directly from the interface of marijuana with the Hypothalamus Control Center known to be responsible for balancing the ANS.

This altered state of consciousness associated with the trophotropic response has been routinely experienced in Eastern and Western cultures...Subjectively it is the experience of ecstasy, clairvoyance, relaxation, peace of mind, sense of well-being. (Bensen)

Studies on meditating Zen masters have shown that the alpha wave mode of this state is one of alert focusing while at the same time complete relaxation or "tranquility," wherein nonverbal information processing or experience of intense meaning predominates.

Music heard so deeply -That it is not heard at all, you are the music, while the music lasts. -T.S. Eliot. "Four Quartets"

The Eastern theory of chakras categorizes states of being according to the vibration of energy that cannot be seen but nevertheless settles at different centers of the human body. Within us we hold the same power as the solar energy of the universe, i.e., the Divine Spark is actually physically encapsulated in our body but is unfulfilled in most lives. You might say, it gets stuck in one of the chakras and never rises to the top.

From the lowest chakra (located at the base of the spine) of unconscious instincts known as the survival center, to the midpoint of self-consciousness at the level of the gut (where ego reigns), there is a natural progression of maturation over the course of a lifetime. It can be likened to the undifferentiated demands of the infant which advances to the ego-driven competitiveness of the normal adult. To rise even further above the usual self-centered consciousness to cosmic consciousness, an additional, intentional push is necessary. It can come by cultivating physical discipline, devotion, and meditation-over a long period of time - practices which are aiming to quiet the mind and foster an attitude of disinterest in self-serving motives. Or the push can come from a plant:

Cultivation, from the Oriental perspective is pursuing a way of life that is more than the average way of life (which) aims at enhancement and perfection of the personality by elevating various capacities of the body-mind from average normality to supernormal standards of thinking and behaving, i.e., there can be no flaw In human sentiments. ((Yuasa)

Refinement from a more highly refined vibration outside oneself can likewise be granted. In the East it is not uncommon for a guru to awaken the aspirant's potential. A guru may be embodied in human form, or may be anything the student is inspired by and considers a teacher -either within, as a mantra, or without, such as music or holy plants. Although the methods of cultivation toward realizing super-normal consciousness have been more precisely defined in the East than anywhere else, understanding and utilizing the experience, as well as practices to apprehend it, are shared by all shamanic traditions.

The heart chakra which loves, and the throat chakra which creates, are the energy centers or states of being that marijuana usually vitalizes. At these levels, the ego is transcended, allowing the higher emotions to come into play. That marijuana can impart the power of higher consciousness is not considered mysterious In the East:

> Plants transmit the vital-emotional impulses, the life-force that is hidden in light. That is the gift, the grace, the power of plants. Plants bring us love, the nourishing power of the sun, which is the same energy of all the stars, of all light. These cosmic energies emanated by plants thus nourish, sustain and ... bring us to the universal light. (Lad)

While marijuana often raises our inner spark of Divine energy to levels of love and creativity, attainment of the highest level of being, Cosmic consciousness requires that a pureness of receptivity be in place. Over time, and with intense cultivation of one's character, marijuana can help us achieve enlightenment. It is only fitting in this age of pollution and plastic that the guru to bless us with Shaktipat comes in the form of an ancient sun-loving plant that has as its most Intrinsic attribute, the power of consciousness raising. The word "Shaktipat" is a combination of Shati (Divine Power) and pat (inspired or awakened by the guru).

The irony of human affairs is that progress toward material pleasure simultaneously diminishes appreciation of the spirit:

> Modern science and business leave no room for God, i.e., for the average man (and woman) there no longer exists anything of meaning and value. (Bonhoeffer)

Our modern technological mindset surely has been exemplary of a culture disinterested in metaphysics, prone instead to material pursuits. This has disintegrated into a deeply felt loss of authentic values and the consequent breakdown of social norms. In this time of synthetic ideals, the great thrust toward the non-transitory virtues that define humanness has predictably led to the natural mind expanding agents. The rush to altered consciousness cannot be stopped.

As it grows toward repression and prohibition, the dominant culture is automatically balanced by an opposing response toward freedom. Yin and Yang of life is a continuous, mobile flux, working always for harmony. Necessity as the mother of invention has moved the impoverished collective of the youth, intelligentsia, the outlawed, and the alienated to ferret out ways to reawaken a sense of meaning to existence. No wonder then that marijuana, the most gentle and effective medicine for relieving chronic anxiety and awakening a profound awe in the "wonder of it all," is ingratiating itself into the natural yearning for the mystical state of extreme wellness.

Enlightenment can be viewed from a number of vantage points: psychologically, it is the experience of no worry, of now-ness, newness and joy: physiologically, the autonomic nervous system is operating at its most balanced state, allowing for full oxygenation of the organism; psychically, it is the connectedness that allows for loving relationships born of seeing beyond the surface, often accentuated by an ability to sense through the constraints of space time; intellectually, it is the moment of revelation, intuition, and creativity; spiritually, the mystic is in a state that transcends all programs.

Since human consciousness can be posited along the continuum of subjective experience, we are able to move upward on the ladder of well-being with the aid of marijuana. We all know this very personal and individual enhancement as "being high" and we also know that we will never give it up.

Science and Cannabis

Ongoing research with Marijuana Therapy has presented the scientific world with some amazing facts. At this time, Cannabis is accepted by the progressive medical community for an enormous number of specific disorders: Spasticity due to spinal cord injury and Multiple Sclerosis; Chronic (especially Neurogenic) Pain; Movement Disorders; Inflammation; Intractable Hiccups; Depression; Anxiety Disorders; Bipolar Disorders; Dependency to Alcohol and Opiates; Alzheimer's Disease; Migraines; In addition to: Glaucoma; Epilepsy; Aids Wasting Syndrome; Certain Cancers: Asthma and Chemotherapy-induced emesis.

Realistically speaking, it is really only a matter of time before the entire medical world embraces the wonders within The Cannabis Sativa Plant.

In fact, the international scientific community is conducting numerous, in-depth investigation into the different constituents of marijuana with extreme diligence in order to extract active ingredients useful for treating particular illnesses. Pharmaceuticalization of this ancient and revered gift of nature is being conducted in hopes of replicating the benefits of the intact plant.

Science is tampering with the selectivity of millions of years in arrogant ignorance of the synergistic realities that attend biological processes. Evolution of the chemical intricacies and similarities in the Plant and Animal Kingdoms has progressed for billions of years. The recently uncovered Cannabinoid System of the animal world has been in existence since the time of the ancient mollusk and so has the Cannabis Sativa Plant. The Cannabinoid System is credited as the modulator, moderator and regulator of all the internal activities in the body, and especially, the processes of brain functioning.

The brain has billions of receptors on millions of neurons. When the right shape molecule floats by the matching receptor, designed by the wisdom of eons of selectivity, there is impact! Unimaginable numbers of interlocking processes are activated. Tampering with the chemical co-compatibility of Cannabis and humans that are born from the same matrix will not reap the balancing wonders that are understood as the benefits of marijuana.

Chapter 7 • BLISS
Anandamide

The Anandamide Story: The Paradox

According to Grinspoon, when medical science looks back onto the discovery of the way in which Cannabis can help the human race, it will be hailed as the "wonder drug of the century!" Anadamide, literally translated as bliss compound is the fat soluble compound made by our brains (and the brains of other animals) which "docks specifically onto cannabinoid receptors" located throughout the entire organism and, as well, in the brain.

(Up until the discovery of Anandamide - at the turn of the century - the only molecule known to fit these receptor sites (discovered just a few years prior) was the THC molecule of the Cannabis Sativa Plant. In fact, it was during experiments trying to decipher the marijuana effect that these ubiquitous receptors were found in the first place. Finding the receptors for which marijuana compounds could impact with great ease led to the discovery of the Cannabinoid Regulatory System that just about balances the whole body.)

Scientists realized that if there were keyholes implanted in the cells, there were also somewhere the keys. The naturally-produced oily "key" produced in the brain was finally located and named for the word "bliss" in the Hindu religions. It was named simply because its action is to impart happiness, well-being, even "bliss," which has since been further defined and understood as the modulating action of balance! Although Anandamide and THC differ in molecular composition, yet an electromagnetic charge or some subtle vibrational identity acts as the Master Key. In this case, Anadamide acts as the key that triggers biochemical changes similar to THC.

The discovery that the bliss experience (too often lost along the journey of stressful living) is actually inherent to the biological make-up of sentient life and can be restored with Cannabis has led to a tremendous surge in research for profit. The goal is to develop "synthetic keys" that can be marketed with the same promise of healing that is inherent to the Master Cannabinoids of the Plant – but without the bliss!

The pharmaceutical attitude is best summarized in the following quote:

> Due to the fact that remarkable curative properties of Cannabis and THC for symptoms such as pain relief, control of nausea and appetite stimulation are mediated by the same receptors as the unwanted psychoactive side-effects their application in medical purposes is limited....major goals of medicinal chemists...to determine structural features required for cannabinoid activity, to optimize medicinal effectiveness and to separate the beneficial effects of cannabinoids from unwanted psychoactive side-effects.
> (Emil Pop, Cannabinoids)

Biochemical destiny, hopefully will help to diminish mainstream fears concerning the unnaturalness of feeling "high" and will aid medical investigators in their search to give needed relief to sick and unhappy people. Some scientists are more rational:

> The "high" associated with marijuana is not generally claimed to be integral to its therapeutic value. But mood enhancement, anxiety reduction, and mild sedation can be desirable qualities in medications particularly for...pain and anxiety. Thus although the psychological effects of marijuana are merely side effects in the treatment of some symptoms, they might contribute directly to relief of these symptoms.
> (Joy JE Watson, (IOM, Assessing the Science Base, 1999)

Children and Marijuana

In Jamaica - where the stigma of marijuana is nearly nonexistent, a very meaningful study has been reported concerning women who ingested the herb while pregnant and the effects it had on the unborn fetus, as well as on the infants whose mothers continued to use marijuana while breast-feeding. The study was under the auspices of the University of Massachusetts Nursing Education Department and published in Pediatrics.

The results were absolutely favorable for the marijuana-exposed babies when compared to the control group of non-exposed infants. This was not really a surprise considering the general health-giving benefits of Cannabis. Jamaica was the locale of preference, specifically because "Scientific reports have documented the cultural integration of marijuana and its ritual and medicinal, as well as recreational functions," thereby disallowing any bias that could contaminate the findings. In areas where marijuana is not socially acceptable, self-reporting of the medicinal herb has not proven reliable owing to the fear of legal and social sanctions. In Jamaica, however, it was also far easier to control all the extraneous factors, such as: "poly-drug use; antenatal care; mother's nutritional status; maternal age; social support as well as the effects of different caretaking environments."

The study was able to control the tobacco and alcohol contamination of other studies previously done in Canada and the U.S. (with conflicting reports) because "marijuana use by women in Jamaica has been relatively uncontaminated by other drugs: even alcohol and tobacco are used only minimally by women."

At the outset, the Jamaican investigation was careful to control for the same type populations among "user" and "non-user," in addition to which "the field workers enjoyed long-standing relationships with the subjects of the test" which the testers told us assured enhanced credibility of the participants' reporting.

The Results

Three days after birth no differences could be detected between the babies of mothers who used marijuana and who did not use marijuana during pregnancy. At one month old, the babies whose mothers ingested marijuana during pregnancy but did not breastfeed "showed better physiological stability, required less examiner facilitation to reach an organized state and become available for social stimulation" (at levels that were definitely statistically significant). And more significantly - at one month old - test results from those babies whose mothers ingested marijuana during pregnancy AND during breast-feeding was "even more striking."

Heavily exposed babies were more socially responsive and more autonomically stable than babies not exposed to marijuana through mother's milk:

> ...alertness was higher; motor and autonomic systems more robust, they were less irritable, less likely to demonstrate imbalance of tone; needed less examiner facilitation to become organized; had better self-regulation; and were judged to be more rewarding for caregivers than the neonates of non-using mothers.

We must examine the outcomes of these tests independent of the study's interpretation since the conclusions of the testers are prone to circuitous reasoning. In the "Discussion" part of the report, the benefits of marijuana on these infants are never mentioned - even though that is what the study was about. Although, at the outset, care was reportedly taken to assure for a nonbiased, balanced sample for the test population, in regard to "status, maternal health, and abstention from other drugs," once the results were tabulated according to double-blind methodology, and once the benefits of marijuana were statistically arranged before their eyes, all manner of rationalities were offered to explain away what was obvious. The testers advanced the theory that perhaps the marijuana-exposed babies' superior functioning was due to the fact that the mothers made up the more educated segment of the study.

Half of these women were made up of marijuana "smokers," which might suggest that they were more independent, etc., thereby giving the babies a different, more attentive type of nurturing. However, and to the disservice of this study, this reasoning is deceiving - it confounds the issue of what "marijuana-use" comprised and who the population was. Although less than half of the mothers "smoked" marijuana (which showed their independence, no doubt), the rest of the traditionally bound Jamaican mothers in the study drank marijuana as a tea - often. This is actually left out of the study's discussion, and one must re-read it to realize the fallacious implication. All the exposed babies, with tea or smoke, were more robust, although the most heavily exposed babies scored the highest (50% of their mothers were among the heaviest smok-ers). When discussing the smoking mothers and the cause of their happier and healthier babies, the authors of the study state that the smoking women were generally in less meaningful relationships with men, or as they put it, there was a "higher level of conjugal instability among users."

At the inception of the study, it is stated: "the heavy marijuana users did not have more income or status than the other women." But during the concluding remarks the testers' reason that without a husband "they (the women who had happier babies) had more control over how they acquired and spent their resources." The way it goes on to read, the results of the study is an advertisement for the ABSENCE of a father (or even a long-standing stable male image), at least in the early stages of life.

> Because they did not rely on male support, they were relatively free to separate and form new relationships if their current relationships were not to their liking.

Throughout this irrelevant discussion, the proven benefits to Health from marijuana-exposure for the infant is forgotten completely, while the authors make a quite convincing argument that fathers and their surrogates represent a liability to the health, responsiveness, and general well-being of infants.

I know that the authors of this investigation worked carefully and scientifically throughout its implementation. They are to be credited with giving us a dose of the truth – even though they tried to hide it. Perhaps if they actually stood by what their study clearly demonstrated, the results might have been "shelved" as in the "update" and we might never have this valuable ammunition in our defense against the Drug War. And perhaps the testers knew that.

Through the cultural traditions given as background in this report, we see that "residents in the rural communities" from which the sample for this study is drawn.

> ...view marijuana not only as a recreational 'drug' but one that has ritual and medicinal value...Marijuana also is known for its therapeutic and health-promoting functions. It is consumed as a tea by family members of all ages for a variety of illnesses and to maintain and promote health (which) ...transcends class, age, and gender divisions.

So we know that - although most women are not smokers of marijuana unless very modern - they almost all drink marijuana tea and give it to their children and elders, and to anyone else who is sick or dejected.

Because the reporters obviously did not want to encourage marijuana use openly for pregnant and nursing mothers, and because the test results were so conclusive while the interpretations were so inconclusive, the last sentence of the published report seems to offer some explanation of the irrationality of the study's confusing conclusion:

> Although some might interpret this failure to identify the relevant variables at the outset...one could argue, conversely, that the projects greatest value is its capacity for discovery and the question of hypothesis and research questions that can be explained in subsequent studies.

As an *adaptogenic* remedy, there is no rationale for keeping the benefits of marijuana from infants, children, or teens. It's "usefulness" for the instabilities suffered so often episodically in; youthful, vibrant organisms, is unsurpassed. For the life-diminishing diseases, such as autism or other non-treatable problems that usually are diagnosed in early childhood, the benefits of Marijuana Therapy are just beginning to emerge via parents who have utilized marijuana as a last resort – which fortunately, revitalized their hopes by affecting their children extremely favorably.

The Future

Ongoing research with Marijuana Therapy has presented the scientific world with some amazing facts. At this time, Cannabis is accepted by the progressive medical community for an enormous number of specific disorders so that realistically speaking it is only a matter of time before the entire world embraces the wonders within Cannabis Sativa. In fact, the international scientific community is conducting numerous, in-depth investigations into the different constituents of the plant with extreme diligence - all the time. The pharmaceuticalization of this ancient and revered gift of nature is well on its way to becoming the new drug of the future. Synthetics and extracts of the plant, known as Cannabis-based medicines, are already in the works, as prescription drugs.

As human beings have evolved from nature – so has the intact, whole marijuana plant. As marijuana was the constant companion of the developing human race throughout history, so has the co-evolution of the chemical intricacies between this vegetable and the human animal progressing since before reported history. Whereas the Cannabis Sativa Plant has been an inhabitant of Planet Earth for nearly 500 million years, humans are newcomers of just a few million years old. The connectivity between the two kingdoms is intimately, historically, chemically, biologically, psychologically and socially intertwined.

To tamper with the co-compatibility of the make-up of the Cannabis Sativa plant and the earth creatures who evolved in its shadow will not reap the balancing wonders that are understood as the benefits of marijuana.

Chapter 8 • The Psychotherapeutic Effects of Marijuana Therapy

What is marijuana therapy for psychological problems?

Marijuana is an ancient herbal superior *adaptogen* which just means it is good for everything.

Adaptogens help the organism to adapt to stress. They maintain and restore balance. They are effective in treating a wide array of diseases. They are sometimes referred to as tonics because they increase vitality. Paradoxically, they can also relax the entire system. There are no dangerous side-effects.

Known in ancient India as the "gift of the gods," marijuana was prescribed as a "reliever of stress."

Until 1990, the way in which marijuana affects the human body was unknown. With the discovery of The Cannabinoid Network and in light of testimonials of thousands of seriously ill patients concerning the relief that marijuana gave them, research into the potential medical applications of the Cannabis plant began in earnest. Over the last few decades and especially following the turn of the century, an unparalleled number of rigorously controlled studies throughout the world has proven, without question, that the effects of Cannabis Sativa are: moderating, modulating and balancing to the human organism.

The legend of marijuana as a panacea for all kinds of physical, psychological and spiritual imbalance has been authenticated by rigorous scientific studies. As further research continues, the potential medical indications for Marijuana Therapy appear boundless. It seems that each month, another widely respectable agency is announcing the results of its carefully documented investigation, demonstrating yet another needed medical application for Marijuana Therapy. So far, test results have shown it to be:

> *"anti-addictive," "anti-aggressive," "anti-allergent," "anti-Alzheimic," "anti-anxiety," "anti-arthritic," "anti-asthmatic," "anti-bacterial," "anti-biotic," "anti-cancerous," "anti-cholesterol," "anti-febrile," and*

"anti-convulsive," "anti-depressant," "anti-diabetic," "anti-exhaustive," "anti-febrile," "anti- hypertensive," "anti-inflammatory," and anti-insomniac," "anti-nauseant," "anti-oxidant," "anti-tumoral," also "anti-spasmodic" and "anti-stroke." In addition, marijuana is a "pain killer," "neuro-protective," a digestive aid, an appetite stimulant, a muscle relaxant, as well as protective against poisonous gas,*" "protective for brain trauma," and a stabilizer of moods.

*The Israeli Army equips soldiers with synthetic marijuana as protection against a Sarin Gas attack – as Cannabis protects the brain in such an event.

Marijuana for Mental Distress

Contemporary thinking divides the human organism into the visible body and the invisible mind. This separation does not really exist but is useful for purposes of discussion and treatment. In fact, each individual is an integration of body, mind and spirit. Without any one of the three components, there is no person. What affects one classification of the individual, affects the whole.

Although manifestations of disease at the level of the physical body are easiest to diagnose and to treat, the actual source of all distress is interwoven throughout the whole person. Whereas marijuana is now a proven and even an acceptable medicine for myriad presentations of imbalance in the physical aspect of personhood, its broad benefits for the mind (known to the ancients thousands of years ago) are only beginning to be uncovered by modern science.

Marijuana Psychotherapy

The effects of marijuana on the body can easily be measured. In Eastern science, the body represents the gross, visible vibration of the person. The mental sphere is of a finer vibration. The spirit is the finest vibration. Whatever affects the gross, corporeal component of the organism - affects as well the whole.

Marijuana balances the Autonomic Nervous System which results in a relaxed alertness. Marijuana regulates the rhythm of the breath, deepens the breathing pattern, expands the capacity of the lungs, and raises the efficiency of the Circulatory System – all of which enhance the overall oxygenation of the organism. The two sides of the brain are synchronized, evidenced by the emanation of Alpha Waves within minutes of administration of marijuana. The sensitivity of all the senses organs is therefore heightened. Perception is sharpened. Mental clarity emerges.

Conventional Psychotherapy
vs.
Marijuana Therapy

The stated goal of psychotherapy is: (1) to increase the general awareness of the patient; (2) to increase understanding of the specific presenting problem for functioning more easily in the world, which in both situations implies lifting the veil of muddy thinking, Yet the traditional approach of "talking therapies" has been mostly unsuccessful. The Freudian "analyzed and the analyzer" process appears logical but, in practice, the incidence of success is low. For an individual, conditioned over a lifetime, to change one's inner, mechanical mental and physical actions has proven resistant to external interventions. The Medical Model tends to elevate the opinion of the expert, fostering passivity in the client which automatically discourages meaningful investigation. In the short run, the directives and expectations of the therapist (regardless of their subtlety) are re-assuring guidelines toward alleviating inappropriate emotions. Over the long term, however, the personality usually reverts back to its familiar dysfunction.

In the last few decades, Psychological Medicine has therefore taken another road. Unfortunately, rather than increasing awareness, Psychiatry has been in the business of simply suppressing the untoward symptoms via pharmacology. In concert with the Pharmaceutical Industry, Psychiatric Medicine has forged an incredibly profitable alliance, as its main treatment modality has become to prescribe drugs as remedial for depression, mood swings, hyperactivity, forgetfulness, insomnia, grief, and other forms of mental distress and confusion, without consideration of cause or life changing remedies.

The Doctors prescribe ever more, newly patented brain-numbing drugs which are ever more subtly damaging to those who will swallow (and can pay). The brain is sedated slightly or its natural chemistry is distorted and then the dosage is adjusted (usually upwards) to a tolerance level below lethality until the bothersome symptoms are no longer evident. Since the person's brain is anesthetized, more unconsciousness (not less) is the result. The drugging of the population, including children and the elderly, has become common, acceptable medical practice which is growing exponentially, fueled by the profit motive to the grave diminishment of intellectual clarity, freedom, creativity, independence and health.

The Philosophy of Holistic Health

Whereas Western "allopathic" medicine works against uncomfortable symptoms without concern for the underlying cause, the Holistic Health approach seeks to locate the source of the problem. Focus is on the whole person and not just on the presenting disturbance. The individual is expected to share in all decisions to alter unhealthy habits so as to approach a level of wellness beyond "not sick." While the Holistic Health model was introduced into Western medicine in the latter half of the twentieth century, it is actually a modern translation of the ancient Oriental philosophies still being practiced today where the goal of life is balance of the physical, mental and spiritual energies of the person. In this model, disease is understood as an expression of imbalance of the whole person, the entirety of which is affected in any attempt at re-balancing.

Different Assumptions in Holistic Health

In complete contrast to the non-participatory dependence advanced by Western Medical Business, Holistic Health is based on the tenets of self-help, self-discipline and self-observation and knowledge. Rather than dealing solely with sickness, holistic philosophy strives for the full measure of well-being which is gauged as a continuum of growth in all facets of the person: body, mind and spirit. Each individual is uniquely valuable with the potential for vital life-experience through increased awareness (not to be in any way treated mechanistically.) Sincere, self-revelatory understanding along with steadfast practice and conscious intention to change one's own way of life can succeed.

Holistic Health assumes that the person in distress is a very interested student/client and also the most active player in determining whatever is causing the problem; and further that he/she is eager to implement lifestyle changes to diminish dysfunction. The participant assumes responsibility for his/her own actions, while the practitioner points out various behaviors to effect change. But the person makes the changes. Long-standing, maladaptive coping mechanisms become exposed through sincere self-examination. With interest, knowledge, patience and self-discipline, healthy alternatives are substituted. The holistic philosophy is a custom-tailored way of living and being, recognizing that everyone is different and has different problems which must be resolved over time. Instantaneous results, as in taking a pill to ward off the symptoms, have no place in the holistic modality.

To undo the habits of years takes time, steadfast interest, as well as a sincere, relentless determination to change.

In Holistic Medicine - Symptoms are not Denied, Repressed, Drugged or Ignored.

Rather than repressing unpleasant symptoms, in Holistic Health, they are treasured clues on the path of becoming aware of the source of imbalance. Conventional psychotherapy deals only with the body/mind components of human life under the theory that the spirit may not exist. Matters of the soul are taboo in Western Medicine which prides itself on its secular discipline. By contrast, the philosophy of Holistic Health acknowledges the primacy of the spiritual dimension in all forms of life. In fact, the ultimate objective of Holistic Medicine is the integration of body, mind and spirit which promises an enhancement of life experience toward joy, happiness and compassion.

Methodology - Effects of Marijuana Therapy

Marijuana Therapy is the practice of Holistic Health by the person! The goal is individualistic in that only the serious and sincere person can determine what is best for him/herself at that moment, and it may well be (and ought to be recognized as) different for everyone. Psychotherapy has often been accused of manipulating the vulnerable patient into comfortable, acceptable societal niches and attitudes that represent the values of the therapist and not the unique needs, make-up and talents of the person.

Whereas modern psychotherapy is founded in the cultural norms of the society, Marijuana Therapy is timeless and without personal bias.

Marijuana Therapy helps to expose fears, belief systems, and ulterior motives through its consciousness-raising quality. The individual, as an interested witness to what is usually denied and hidden, then has the potential to transcend the conditioning of years, and possibly for discovering who one really is. With Marijuana Therapy, there is a basic uncoupling from all that has been imbedded into the psyche/soma by the reigning value base.

Rather than Authoritarian
Marijuana Therapy is Autonomous

The outer-directed person is concerned with the judgments of others, whereas inner-direction is driven from the very essence of the individual. Unfortunately, those who march to their own unique beat are, by definition not in sync with the mainstream. Through the *marijuana experience*, everlasting, meaningful ideals are often crystallized leading to a philosophical understanding that rises above the cultural norm of personal pleasure and may well effect lasting changes in the receptive personality toward more altruistic behavior. With successful Marijuana Therapy, the individual is more integrated in his/her fundamental nature; and therefore less conflicted and more at ease. In addition, inner strength will naturally develop through the continuous realization of intuitive righteousness.

Rather than Public
Marijuana Therapy is Private

Owing to the confounded rationale presented for the legal restraints against marijuana and the subsequent mystique that necessarily is created from "what is forbidden" for no good reason, Marijuana Therapy often takes place not only privately but oftentimes secretly. In a private setting, without the distraction of talking or any other kind of personal interaction, the serenity of mind and relaxation of body that is common to the *marijuana experience* allows for deep self-understanding which can cause changes in perceptions and behavior. Selfish motives and values that have been sanctioned by the materialistic culture are often exposed; in their place, higher ideals of compassion may be assumed which unfortunately can be contrary to the welfare of the individual in this competitive world.

Marijuana Therapy is Transforming Not Conforming

Conforming:

Modern Psychotherapy is deemed successful if the patient learns to accept and to conform to the social norms and goals. Questioning culturally accepted mores is not encouraged because it is not relevant to the objective of becoming productive and well-adjusted in accordance with the expectations of the larger community. To conform to the conditions as they exist and not rail against them is the practical, sought-after attitude in the psychotherapeutic model. Constant complaining of not being able or willing to find a suitable niche for oneself within society implies deviance or neurosis.

The old-fashioned character ideals - held in high regard just a few generations ago, such as inner strength, independent thinking, moral principles and conscientious service are no longer of interest and in no way within the guidance given by psychotherapists. In the fast-paced, materialistic philosophy, power, wealth and recognition supersede time-honored objectives. The goals and methods of psychotherapy are in tune with the population. To consider that an individual with confused thinking, low energy and irrational fears may be suffering from lack of spiritual cultivation is not imaginable as a diagnosis nor is there any known psychiatric remedy. Instead obsessive behaviors, swings in moods, destructive eccentricities are identified as chronic, involuntary chemical imbalances, and cavalierly treated with drugs. Conforming is thereby facilitated since the symptoms have been anesthetized, along with the consciousness. The personality has been sedated (or slightly deadened), which suggests a loss in intensity of experience as well as a diminished depth of response. Therapy is deemed successful because the original, presenting issues have also become less bothersome (with depressant drugs) and are quietly tucked back into the subconscious of the weakened person.

Regardless that modern "therapies," state the goal of the psychotherapeutic process as geared to increasing awareness, unless the spiritual dimension is acknowledged and cultivated, there is no movement toward (or even recognition of) the extensive evolution in consciousness available to the human being. By not addressing the energizing principle that courses through all that exists, current medicine is deficient at its foundation. In this respect it has progressed to an incomplete science, having lost the pre-modern understanding of the primacy of the spirit in all healings.

To Be Transformative
Marijuana Therapy Mandates Intentionality

In those cases, where marijuana is utilized purely as a recreant, the therapeutic value of marijuana will not reach to the inner make-up of the individual. Although extremely healthy for body and mind, Marijuana Therapy does not take hold as a sacramental experience, without the intention to grow in esoteric understanding.

Transforming:

So it is that in this dark age of materialism - there is a natural turning toward the marijuana mind which harkens back to an authentic familiarity of higher ideals that invites evolution of the spirit. An all encompassing enthusiastic attitude of well-being takes hold through the fuller, deeper, slower, quieter, more effortless way of breathing that is the natural counterpart of Marijuana Therapy. Owing to the increased oxygenation of the whole organism, mental confusion dissolves into a calm, less egocentric thought pattern, evidenced in the synchronicity of the brain hemispheres demonstrating "Alpha" patterns with the administration of marijuana. The measurable slowing down (of the frames) in thinking results in greater attentiveness to each thought. (The subjective experience of increased awareness, commonly referred to as "being high" is produced through the natural affinity of Cannabis compounds to specific and ancient receptors in the brain.) Rather than less energy, there is more. This result is liberation not limitation of the personality.

Spiritual cultivation is an intentional process that can only begin from a balanced, positive perspective. Marijuana Therapy produces a natural re-stabilizing of the entire organism which sets the stage for transformation of the personality. The clarity imparted by marijuana (owing to the physiological effects that can be measured) allows one to rise above the expectations of the conditioning. According to McKenna: The plant hallucinogens dissolve habits and hold motivations up to inspection by a wider, less egocentric, and more grounded point of view..

While the food chain expresses the transfer of energy between different organisms in a concrete and visible way, the chain of consciousness is conveyed in the inner world of the recipient - invisible to the uninterested, untrained eye. The energetic transfer of the more powerful plants of consciousness is intense and abrupt. Hidden agendas, repressed fears and universal realities that are almost always filtered from awareness come bursting forth, shocking the personality with naked truth. Rarely, a total transformation in the personality can occur evidenced by lasting liberation from personal worry and an abiding empirical knowledge that all is right in the universe. This can only happen if the organism is able to withstand the enormous jolt of reality. Usually the magnitude of the alteration in consciousness fades with time; its meaning becomes less immediately accessible to memory. Explorations with the powerful visionary plants are almost always time-spaced journeys by virtue of the incredible strength of the experience and the need to re-stabilize to be able to withstand and appreciate once again the powerful charge.

Marijuana Therapy is Long-term, Gentle and NOT an Immediate Fix

In contrast, the effects of marijuana are gentle, slower, more digestible, and most importantly - easily integrated into the awareness of daily living. Marijuana Therapy is cumulative and hierarchical in that over time the subject slowly gains ascendancy on the ladder of spiritual growth so that each new understanding builds upon the plateau of learning beneath it. The transformation from worry and self-centered concern to acceptance and compassion is incremental, subtle and gradual.

Marijuana Therapy is Magnetic, Life-Long and Choiceless

Marijuana Therapy is lifelong reflection for the purpose of attaining to an energetic vibration of purity. It is not enlisted for a specific time frame to alter a personality-driven problem. Instead, the objective is transformation of the whole organism through the increased energy of awareness. Although there is no perfection on the way to spiritual truth, there is no cessation of searching. In truth, Marijuana Therapy is a choiceless response to the magnetic pull for realizing states of being of a higher energetic charge than is usual for the common person. Marijuana imparts empirical evidence of a reality beyond the mundane. Once apprehended, it cannot be ignored. If not experienced, no words can describe it.

When the exogenous cannabinoids of the Cannabis plant have merged with the organism, a transformation occurs in the actual operational competence of the whole person. This is demonstrated by the limitless mental and physical dysfunctions that are ameliorated with the administration of marijuana. The eyes really do see better, the ears hear more tones, touch is sensitized, the mind field is focused, and of course, taste is enhanced. There is fuller breath, greater relaxation, better circulation, improved digestion and elimination, and superior neuro-protectiveness. Tolerance is increased, appreciation grows, and awareness is broadened. In addition, perceptions are heightened and a deep compassion may emerge. These effects of marijuana are experienced subjectively and are physically demonstrable.

It is this mystical awareness imparted in the *marijuana consciousness* that (can) transform(s) one's entire outlook on life over the long term. But for evolution toward higher development to take place (by which is meant a deepening awareness of inner motivations, as well as extending concern for all earth creatures), "intentionality" is required. This implies purposeful, steadfast determination to tread the path of growth in the spirit.

While there is no doubt that Marijuana Therapy has inherent health benefits for the physical and mental components of the human organism, spiritual evolution is not assured. Although humans have the potential to realize states of being beyond normal self-concerned consciousness, in actuality there is no biological or psychological necessity for such a transformation to be realized other than personal longing.

The yearning for deeper understanding is not innate to everyone. According to the esoteric lore of the East, there is a time of karmic ripening whereby an individual is drawn intuitively to seek out knowledge of that which is not transitory. In the Fourth Way Tradition, this stage of readiness is known as the "Magnetic Center." Marijuana Therapy can serve as a vehicle by which timeless and eternal ideals and insights unfold, in addition to allowing for personal examination of the inner workings of the mind. It is in this capacity that marijuana is uniquely beneficial in that it fulfills the particular need of the individual: physical, psychological and spiritual..

Marijuana Group Therapy

Because the social outlook today is so far removed from any cultivation or even recognition of alternative states of being, the assemblage of the marijuana community serves as a point of reference to share and validate common perceptions and judgments of the mystical effects familiar to the experiences with marijuana. By coming together in energetic harmony during the *marijuana consciousness*, a sense of camaraderie is produced, allowing for spontaneous discussion concerning the otherworldly intuitions that present with higher states of awareness - which cannot be easily discussed in conventional circles. The stigma of marijuana has actually helped to cement together those (of us) who would dare to deviate from culturally accepted proscriptions.

"Meditation-in-Action" & Marijuana Therapy

The *marijuana consciousness* is the still point in the midst of confusion.

In the 16th Century, Shakespeare said, "The world is too much with us." What better way to describe the never ending hustle and bustle of life in the 21rst Century. To be busy constantly and to socialize with other people as much as possible is encouraged, expected and easily accomplished in this age of communication. Plans, worries, hopes and fears fill our minds. Entertainment, telephones, televisions and computers are always there to take up "empty" time. We are taught from the beginning that idleness is wrong while being alone is boring. In other words, the society is based on continuous planning, productivity and activity. From bright colored-mobiles for the day old infants to senior activities for the dying, no allowance exists for doing nothing. There is no time for restoration or rebalancing of the organism – unless, of course, one is to practice Marijuana Therapy.

Regardless of the situation, the *marijuana consciousness* abides. It allows for noticing one's thoughts during all the activities of life. In this respect, it is a supreme aid for "meditation-in-action." By the energy sharing that takes place between the human organism and the exogenous cannabinoids, the innumerable self-concerned thoughts that pass through the mind are exposed and registered. Personal self-esteem issues, survival worries, future fears can be viewed objectively and resolved more easily when in a reflective mode. Relationship-problems are understood more clearly since the *marijuana experience* can be likened to taking a deep breath. Stress is relieved through the physiological and psychological effects of Marijuana Therapy which neutralizes the pressure inherent in daily living. Fuller breathing sets the stage for rationality rather than impetuous, "acting out." Meditation-in-action is the state of being in the world but not of it. The *marijuana consciousness* is the still point in the midst of confusion.

Unless there is the intention to grow in the spirit, the benefits of marijuana will be limited to the physical and psychological dimensions.

WHO CAN BENEFIT FROM MARIJUANA THERAPY?

The Question Should Be:
WHO CANNOT BENEFIT FROM MARIJUANA THERAPY?

At the end of the 20th century, the long-standing mystery of how marijuana affects the human being was finally discovered. Actually how the Cannabinoid Network remained hidden from microscopic probing - even though it is a ubiquitous physical presence in all mammalian organs, cells and systems - is an even bigger mystery, especially considering that the Cannabinoid Network is vital to the operational efficiency of life. Further scientific research has demonstrated that this ancient, sophisticated, cellular Communication System "regulates, moderates, and modulates the automatic processes in the organism.

The cannabinoid receptors, along with the endogenous-cannabinoids (produced in the brain) comprise the Cannabinoid Network. According to recent studies, communication amongst the receptors via the cannabinoids is nearly instantaneous - sometimes working in a unique order so that it appears there is a magical ability to predict what messages will be sent before they actually are. The whole person experience of well-being that is reminiscent of childhood may very well be nothing more than a properly functioning Cannabinoid System which maintains equilibrium in the body, the breath patterns and the mind through its built-in electro-magnetic signaling of toning down extreme reactions and energizing lethargic states. Perceptions are clear, emotions pure and responses honest when the person is optimally charged.

For every creature on the planet, life represents challenge. With the difficulties and disappointments that occur naturally over time, balance can be compromised, energy dissipated and experience diminished. When a whole race displays ever-mounting incidence of physical and psychological chronic illness (dis-ease), the mechanism for stability within the collective (and continuance of the specie) is corrupted.

Society has lost the basic self-regulating element of humanness. Through the encouragement of constant competition, the natural component that evolved within our beings over millennia specifically to maintain equanimity has been over-worked. As a result, all levels of illness have developed - from insanity to chronic disease and including collective murder. Human nature is not strong enough for the continuous struggle to uphold image, money, power. Humans are "three-brained-beings" (body, mind and soul), according to the Persian Sage Gurdjieff. With a physical overload of stimulating chemicals, the signature of a goal-oriented world, the body degrades and balance is shaken. Stress (imbalance) results in mental and physical sickness which precludes being able to witness or "know" the mystery of life that is within.

The Cannabinoid Network is a systemic gyroscope that has become exhausted through the "excess" of continuous, extreme over-stimulation and resultant depression. Marijuana Therapy is the natural, compatible, gentle, safe, ancient, time-tested and easily available method for returning to the relaxed outlook of childhood, hopefully with the evolved adult ability to appreciate the accompanying higher consciousness. The adaptogenic excellence of the sun-loving Cannabis plant defines its versatility and safety as well as its kindness. Whatever disequilibrium exists, on whatever plane the distortion manifests, regardless of age, frailness, ailment, gender, prior medical history or bias – the energy transference that is given to the human organism by the sun-imparting Herb releases the tension and restores balance. The therapeutic value of marijuana is homeopathic in that whatever / wherever the disturbance is located, that is the locale at which the remedial action will serve.

However, Marijuana Therapy is **Not Recommended**:

For those - disinterested and/or overly dismayed by personal self-centered motives beneath the surface and the fear that drives those motives, greater awareness of unconscious issues cannot be integrated.

For those - well-defended in their fears, without yearning for states of being beyond the mundane, Marijuana Therapy will not awaken the spiritual realm. The physical and psychological release that usually accompanies marijuana, may prove disorienting, without appreciable health advantages since the person will actually ward off the liberating and unfamiliar and therefore dangerous aspects of marijuana. For these character-types, marijuana is frightening in the intensity of its clarity.

For those who are propagandized by the misinformation concerning Marijuana Therapy and feel secure in their ignorance, there is little hope to plumb the depths of their prejudice. They too will not be able to receive the energetic charge of marijuana for at first hint of deep breathing and therefore a "reality check," the body and mind will contract, rather than allow for expansion.

Chapter 9 • Paranoia vs. Well-being

Anxiety caused by Marijuana
Anxiety eliminated with Marijuana

The link between anxiety and marijuana demonstrates the intimate interaction between thinking and breathing.

In the West the connection between breathing and the world of subjective experience is overlooked. But in the East, the intricate relationship between thoughts, breath patterns and body functions has been studied for thousands of years. In fact, whole lifetimes can be and have been spent by accomplished masters and their students investigating the infinite subtleties of Prana or (what is meant by) "breath." According to the most basic understanding in The Science of Yoga, the body, the mind, and the subtle energy in the breath are just different densities of the Singular vibratory essence of the universe. This profound recognition of the unity of cosmic manifestation runs throughout the entire fabric of the Eastern perspective, not limited to philosophical abstractions but interwoven in the practicalities and practices of everyday existence.

The Yogic Model in Medicine

The natural system of Holistic Medicine that has been practiced in India for over 5000 years is termed Ayurveda, translated as *knowledge of life*. It has as its oath not just to minister to the body but to work toward harmony of the physical, psychological and spiritual energies that comprise the individual. Through extensive, deep, long-term interest and study, the Yogic Medical Model has determined that the nuances in the unique "pattern of the breath" of each person are (directly and verifiably) responsible for the differences in experience, including feelings, health, and levels of consciousness.

What is the Meaning of "The Breath"

The Indian word, "Prana" describes the life force of creation. In the English language, there is really no equivalent term to explain the myriad functions, joys, cosmological, biological, chemical and vibrational interactions and states of being that are ascribed to Prana. Because of its vast, varied, eternal and intricate meanderings as the creative force, a devout holiness is attributed to Prana. It is the *giver of life*, the sustainer of all that is manifest. Any translation of Prana as "the breath" must include within its connotation the recognition that pure consciousness is encapsulated in that meaning. When Prana is subsumed within the human being, it serves as the invisible link between body and mind. According to the teachings of Yoga Science, full integration between the physical and mental components of human life is the path to superior health and awareness. Deep, effortless, regular breathing patterns signal relaxation in body and serenity of mind. By contrast, worry consists of a shallow, fast, non-rhythmic breath pattern and implies less than full health (undernourishment by Prana).

"The breath," is not just the way a person takes in gases and expels them. Instead, the intricate details of how fast, how much, how effortlessly, how silently the gases are taken in, how well they circulate, i.e., how smoothly, rhythmically, regularly, quietly and deeply - the Prana flows - all this and so much more is implied in "The Breath." There is also included how the organs function in relationship to the pattern of the breath, how individual muscles respond, how nerves are regulated, and how the entire autonomic (automatic) systems in the body are functioning; and including how clear are the perceptions, judgments, feelings and actions.

The great promise of Yoga is that the mind, with all its levels of complexities, can actually be quieted via healthy breathing. Breathing patterns, although deeply ingrained within the personality, can be improved with knowledge and training, which translates as enhanced life experience. The breath connection affects both physical and mental health. And fortunately, the reverse is equally true. Thought patterns affect breathing which affects body integrity. Yoga Science teaches that to channel the mind is nearly impossible because the mind is so quick and so restless, but to enhance and expand the pattern of breathing is quite possible with determination and assiduous practice. In turn, the mind will follow.

Marijuana was utilized by yogic sages specifically for its enhancement of *the breath*.

The Natural vs. The Conditioned Breath

In the last few decades, the wisdom of Yoga has been filtering into the West via Alternative Medicine and Holistic Health. These disciplines recognize the need for effortless full breathing as the main prescription for health, happiness and spiritual realization. While newborns breathe with calm, regular, full and noiseless constancy, this naturally uninhibited pattern of the breath inevitably becomes restricted over the course of normal life. Perceived and real threats, physical and psychological, stymie the personality, paralleled automatically in irregularities of the breath. The easy signature of baby-breathing is no longer so in the average adult.

Protective body postures and mental defense mechanisms develop through chronic pressure and these coping strategies become habitual over the course of normal stress-filled living. The whole organism develops a defensiveness, which is known as "armor" in psychological jargon. The armor or tension in the muscles is often visible to the trained eye. Massage, drugs, and meditation are all methods that can help to restore relaxation to the organism. Then the breath becomes full, the body relaxed and there is little or no mental chatter. There is a sense of freedom and well-being. (Unfortunately, modern stressors are reaching even into the youth - evidenced with the rise of constitutional asthma among younger and younger children.)

In neurotic personalities, worry predominates. Defense mechanisms rule. The breath is chronically contracted. There is an overall aura of restrictedness, a tendency to hold back from relationships, to hold in feelings, and, most importantly, to inhibit the breath, all in the service of denying the painful past. It becomes more comfortable to breathe less deeply because then there is less vulnerability and more control to avoid anxious feelings. The chronically restricted breather acclimates to a life that is less free, less spontaneous and less creative. While burying what is painful is a common coping mechanism, it is unhealthy, both physically and mentally. Buried emotions smolder in the unconscious and are the source of anxiety. In addition, holding in the anxiety steals energy from vital processes, resulting in negative thoughts and feelings.

Although avoiding anxiety is the unconscious goal, the trade-off is a prescription for sickness. Modern stress-related chronic disease and also the full spectrum of mental disorders, with all their abbreviated symbols, such as ADD, AHAD, GAD, SAD, ETC. are basically expressions of breathing dysfunction. Breath affects everything: how we think, how we meet challenges, how our body chemistry operates, whether toxins are removed or stored, even how effectively our heart beats.

The Conditioned Breath is Persistent

Marijuana Therapy releases constriction in the breath, instantly, gently, reliably, and safely without numbing the person.

To free the blockage in the conditioned pattern of the breath by sheer will is not possible. The muscles are rigid and the chest cavity cannot even accommodate to greater breath. The lungs do not (and cannot) let go of the staleness. In addition, the mind is likewise conditioned. Changing the depth of respiration, the rhythm and smoothness of breathing, changes all aspects of the person including one's belief system which is understandably resisted, and feared. The taut muscles, the shallow, uneven breath, and the limited mind all share in keeping painful vulnerabilities at bay, and are representative of a *narrow-minded* perspective, which clings to the status quo for validation and security. The experience that accompanies such a protected personality is anxiety.

In Western Medicine the main prescription for anxiety is to numb the awareness through anesthetizing drugs so that the patient no longer feels the discomfort. The source of the problem is not ferreted out, instead the symptom is treated. Marijuana Therapy works, instead to uncover the problem in an atmosphere of more (not less) awareness. With the increased capacity and depth of breath as an immediate and constant of marijuana, there is an opening of the entire personality, as in open-mindedness. Marijuana Therapy is an accelerated (and ancient) aid to health via the direct benefits it affords the breath. With the help of the Cannabis Sativa plant, which has been utilized to relieve distress for thousands of years, anxiety can be dissolved.

Marijuana Therapy can become a lifelong healthful habit, continuously restoring the capacity for vulnerability.

Methods: Health of Body/Mind & Spirit
Lessening the Anxiety – Loosening the Armor

With Marijuana Therapy, a gentle, almost immediate expansion in the capacity of the lungs takes place as the alveolar dilate allowing for greater gas exchange and deeper, more rhythmic breathing. Expansion in the capacity of the lungs is likewise facilitated owing to relaxation in the oppositional muscles of the chest. The lungs, which have now greater ability to inflate, in fact now have the room to expand into that increased capacity. Blood vessels are dilated so that less resistance exists in the channels for carrying nourishment throughout the body. As the breathing pattern is deepened, there is an accompanying slowing down in the rate of the pattern of the breath which quite automatically decreases the speed of unconscious thinking. The mind is quieted. More attention can be paid to each topic, since the frames of thought processes are measurably slowed. The greater synchronicity of the brain evidenced in increased alpha rhythm is the exact opposite of the state of anxiety. The net effect is one of calm alertness.

During Marijuana Therapy, anxiety is released along with the overall tension of the organism. In the process of the relaxation that takes place, energy is freed and armor is melted. The material that was buried is no longer hidden. It has become exposed for examination with greater awareness and rationality, since the brain is working more effectively, having been fueled with more oxygen. (That is - the blood can flow better throughout the non-constricted blood vessels, and the blood that does flow is more efficiently oxygenated, owing to the deepening and fullness of the breathing mechanism. In fact, it could be argued that the brain itself is actually expanded.)

It is said that Prana rides on the breath. The flow of the life sustaining energy is quickened via the total body/mind response of Marijuana Therapy. Inhalation and exhalation become naturally quiet because obstructions in the nasal passages are eliminated, either through capillary dilation and/or relaxation of the facial muscles, and including the anti-inflammatory effects of Marijuana Therapy.

Marijuana Therapy results in breathing with more fullness, more depth, and more regulation which registers as relief from tension (in the body/mind) and therefore a lessening of anxiety.

The Inherent Magnetism to Health

The persistent global magnetism to marijuana is none other than the intrinsic human drive to health and happiness. "Getting high," is the experience of intensified awareness wherein the breath is liberated, the body relaxed and the mind released from its constant straining. Restoring stability to the organism back to where it would be if there had not been the challenges and disappointments of life allows for the lost emotion of wonder. Nevertheless, as a remedy for undue amounts of blocked energy, Marijuana Therapy can be a two edged sword.

Paranoia – the Quickening of Anxiety

Rarely, in a minority of people with excessive anxiety, Marijuana Therapy unleashes a cascade of unpleasant memories. Rather than a gentle, slow and easy expansion, the release of pent-up energy is abrupt. An immense amount of denied emotional content is simultaneously presented to consciousness. The *paranoid reaction* implies that the extreme, chronic rigidity in the breath has been released, thus freeing a reservoir of hidden fears which have become exposed to the heightened awareness of the *marijuana experience*. The reality is overwhelming. *To Know Oneself* is the goal, but for the subtly suffocated organism, to leave one's comfort zone is frightening.

The dilemma: *either* remain in stagnation where there is familiar safety; *or* withstand the distress of losing one's defense mechanisms with the possibility for freedom in the personality. (Or there is the Medical Model's *third* choice of depressants for further unconsciousness.) The *paranoid reaction* fortunately fades within a few hours. The mental and physical armor re-establishes itself. But not completely! If the door to consciousness has been opened, it cannot ever be completely closed. Marijuana Therapy is an opportunity to breathe fully and to see clearly. With mindful titration of marijuana, over time, the increased energy is more easily tolerated as full breathing and its enhanced sensitivity becomes familiar, comfortable, even enjoyable. Hitherto denied problems are exposed to the light of intelligence, and are understood and overcome. The personality has begun to grow.
As a lifelong healthful habit, Marijuana Therapy continuously restores the capacity for vulnerability.

Chapter 10 • PTSD and Marijuana Therapy

PTSD Defined:
Severe, debilitating and long-standing psycho-physical dysfunction with intense episodic eruptions that derives from terrorizing, de-humanizing and traumatizing experience that destabilizes the entire organism.

What Causes PTSD ?

The extraordinary shock to the entire organism that results in PTSD has a mental component as well as a physical counterpart. Contrary to secular science, there is also a spiritual, life-affirming value that is compromised in the PTSD. Since the habit of restricting the breath becomes a constant, yet nearly-invisible addendum to the way the person perceives and presents to the world, by releasing the chronically constricted breathing pattern, Marijuana Therapy aids in all aspects of life-experience and is recommended for all types of characterological anxiety-disorders. Post Traumatic Stress Disorder - however, is not a characterological disorder of chronic anxiety formed throughout the developing years. Instead it is a result of just a single (or a cluster of) event(s) that is perceived as it is in progress by the victim as an "unspeakable terror." PTSD is actually a wounding which fails to heal at the emotional level. While the wound inflicted by the horrific event is not visible, what has been measured in PTSD victims are changes in specific cellular communication in the brain and in the hyped-up irregularity of the breath.

Who Gets PTSD ?

The victim need not have had any noticeable psychological distress before the unspeakable horror that caused PTSD, although some studies suggest that the very young or old are more vulnerable, and that anxiety disorders and depression may also be contributing factors. On the other hand, the victim may very well have been highly functioning, without even the tendency toward neurotic behavior. According to recent scientific studies, during the circumstance that caused PTSD, there is a shock of such magnitude that it destabilizes the balancing mechanisms of the organism. When a person witnesses an event that is so atrocious to his/her own sensibilities (even if it is inflicted on someone else) as to elicit the most feared of all possibilities: one's own death, the core inability to accept that final inevitability is triggered. Whether the precipitating trauma is a danger to the continued integrity of the body or threatens the entire personal belief system, the intense reaction is often followed by PTSD.

Although the circumstances may be equally horrendous, the perception of the event is what results in PTSD or Not

Although PTSD is an "event" based dysfunction, certain people are more vulnerable to developing it than others. Right-brained, present-oriented personalities have the highest susceptibility. They experience the world-at-large emotionally, from a sensory basis. During the precipitating event, these personality types withstand the full force of the trauma without even imagining escape. They are trapped in the experience at all levels of experience. Left-brained personalities, by contrast, are linear, with energy expended habitually on future possibilities. Even in the midst of an "unspeakable horrow," the linear-styled personality is considering how to escape and the future. Therefore part of the energy devoted to the experience of horror is dissipated. The emotion-based person is completely engrossed in the present sensory moment of terror – with no distraction, so that he/she ingests the greatest burst of shocking material. It is interesting to note that right-brain and left brain tendency can be determined by the (Lateral Eye Movements) direction in which people look when answering certain questions. In working with PTSD - beings new sufferers, one of the novel treatment modalities that holds promise is working with eye movements of the patients by having them follow direction from the physician's hand. By re-training the LEM habit, the traumatic event becomes less intense, suggesting that brain functioning follows or is directly correlated to eye movement, so that the habituated engrained fear reactivity is short-circuited by interruption of the usual LEM.

Symptoms of PTSD

Following the "event," instead of returning to normal balance, the organism remains in a state of Sympathetic overload. Hyper-vigilance and hyperactivity do not give way to the normalcy of a dynamic re-steadying. The diagnosis of chronic PTSD follows a three-month period of waiting to see whether or not the organism re-rights itself or maintains its "wired" mode. To be wired is to have an explosive energetic charge, just beneath the surface which is easily recognized externally by an interested observer. Subjectively, the person is relentlessly alert, on guard and suspicious which leads to confusion, rage, restlessness, depression, exhaustion, and manifestation of illness in the body – the result of continuous over-stimulation.

The emergence of PTSD flashbacks is episodic and can be triggered by any sense-perception, so that even a certain odor can precipitate re-living the trauma, with all the accompanying acute fight or flight reactions, since the person is actually experiencing the horrendous memory with total emotional recall and precise intellectual details.

Because the potential for the dreaded flashback is ever present, victims of PTSD have a tendency to avoid situations that have the possibility of triggering the memory – which are many and many are unpredictable. Continuous avoidance of people, places and things is often the habitual mechanism adopted for coping with PTSD resulting in diminished life-experience, detachment from close associations, and a low affect suggestive of loss of feeling. Although it appears that emotions are absent, in fact, there is a constant holding back of nervous bottled-up energy that causes sleep disturbance, inability to concentrate, general irritability, an exaggerated startle reflex, and irrational bursts of anger.

The Physiological Manifestation of PTSD

Science has been able to determine that different types of experiences are actually filed in specific areas of the brain. With PTSD, the memory of the horrible event is stored in the *amygdala* (pre-verbal) part of the brain, which is in charge of sensory input and feelings. These memories are emotional without intellectual analysis and therefore demonstrate as a purely gut reaction.

Normally, painful and threatening memories remain in the background, fading over time; and are only called forth in periods of danger, when they serve the survival instinct. At that moment, the person can react solely from the imbedded fear-based experience - instinctively, without thought. With PTSD, however, the memory does not fade! It is vivid and always can resurface in its original intensity. During the trauma, the person is subjected to an unexpected brunt of energy experienced as an immediate, direct and life-threatening assault to life (or to the personal belief system) which results in an actual organic rearrangement of neuronal connections within the *amygdala region of the brain*.

The Amygdala – To Remember vs. To Forget

The amygdala is not an organ but groupings of specially-shaped cells of grey matter buried deep in the primitive Limbic System of the brain that deals with emotional recall. Dangerous memories are stored through cellular and molecular changes in the amygdala. Whenever there is a perceived peril which has been encoded to memory - the Sympathetic Nervous System is activated to the *fight or flight* mode by directorship from the amygdala. The amygdala is divided into sections or areas which serve different functions and respond to different stimuli. Smell, reflex-readiness and releasing appropriate brain hormones as protection to the organism are all within the realm of amygdala activity.

Whether by sound, smell, touch, taste, hearing or thought, PTSD is a disorder that erupts whenever the stored, unconscious, physically imbedded memories break through to the conscious mind without any reference to time or locale. In other words, the memory feels like it is taking place in the here and now, with exactly as much sensory input as when it actually did occur. This present orientation is the basic problem.

Usually, without the destabilization that occurs in PTSD, terrifying events are tucked back into awareness, to be called forth instead with an intellectual, verbal, analytic and narrative memory, wherein the emotional component has been mostly forgotten.

Not To Be Able To Forget Is PTSD
How Marijuana Helps

Although Marijuana Therapy has evidenced extremely positive results in cases of the various classifications of anxiety disorders by its balancing of the ANS and its expansion/ regulation in the breathing capacity - an additional and specific manner in which Cannabis impacts the organism to ameliorate the syndrome of continuous (Sympathetic hyper-arousal) imbalance of the ANS and classified as PTSD has been discovered:

Aversive conditioning, such as pain which fades over time in normal situations, will not fade or become forgotten if the Cannabinoid Networks of the amygdala are malfunctioning or absent. In other words, for the *mechanism of forgetting* to be in proper working order, the cannabinoid receptors, the brain hormones to which the receptors bind, as well as the electro-magnetic signaling that is produced during the impactions must all be operational. The fact that the Cannabinoid Network is instrumental in filtering out from consciousness that which is detrimental to present orientation was discovered through recent research. Experiments were conducted wherein cannabinoid receptors were removed from animal brains resulting in the animals not being able to forget the associations of pain as were the animals in the control. That is, removal of cannabinoid receptors in the amygdala area of the brain did not allow the animals to forget the trauma inflicted upon them, regardless of the time passed or the attempts at re-conditioning. Without the Cannabinoid System's inherent response to over-stimulation within the amygdala, the mechanism for forgetting is lost.

In PTSD, the area of the brain that usually allows the normal person not to remember painful events and therefore not to relive those events, shuts down. The individual who has experienced the degree of terror necessary to cause such a disruption in the brain's *"mechanism of forgetting"* (which of course is unique to everyone's make-up) now constantly remembers. Malfunction in the cannabinoid reception of the endogenous (naturally produced brain) cannabinoids can be ascribed to two possibilities. (1) The receptors are not able to integrate the natural cannabinoids because they are malfunctioning or limited in number/efficiency; (2) less than required endogenous cannabinoids are being produced/released. Either situation results in the continued state of hyper-arousal with the resulting dysfunction.

Conventional Therapy:

In order to jump start the non-functioning *"mechanism for forgetting,"* counseling falls short since intellection alone cannot impact the physical disorganization within the physical brain. To numb or tranquilize the brain's ability to remember – which is the Medical Model's first line of defense against PTSD - is non-specific therapy which is responsible for less than full alertness throughout the entire organism. In conventional psychiatric treatment, in order to be able to forget the terror, total recall is compromised. Once the brain is anesthetized, however slightly, there exists the dumbed - down personality which cannot experience life at its fullest.

Marijuana Therapy is Specific:

Marijuana Therapy impacts the amygdala part of the brain very specifically through a sophisticated mechanism of chemical inter-relationships. Since it has been determined that in cases of PTSD, either the cannabinoid receptors are not working efficiently or the endogenous cannabinoids are lacking in some respect, by administering exogenous (plant) cannabinoids, the re-awakened Cannabinoid System restores the amygdala to an operational mode. Hyper-vigilance is toned down, balance is returned. According to scientific research, the cannabinoid receptors demonstrate a special affinity for plant cannabinoids, in preference to endogenous cannabinoids. It has been shown that the cannabinoid receptors embrace the compounds of Cannabis Sativa with more enthusiasm than they do the brain's own custom-tailored-hormones.

The Benefits of Self- Medicating with Marijuana Therapy

Considering the numbers of citizens suffering from PTSD, the moral mandate for a culture is to provide the most effective treatment.
Including rape victims, combat soldiers and childhood abuse, estimates of Americans suffering from PTSD in any given year are over ten million, with military personnel who served in Iraq scoring the highest percentage to date (Between 12% to 20%). Although combat has always been faulted for causing PTSD – which years ago was known as "shell-shock," the numbers of soldiers with PTSD during modern war-fare has risen to nearly 30% owing to the constancy of being on guard in situations of mass destruction and human maiming with no time away

from the extreme danger. Estimates are probably below the actual number of those suffering from PTSD since so many cases are either un-reported or under-diagnosed.

Self-medication with Marijuana Therapy: Promise for PTSD victims

One of the most important characteristics of Cannabis is how fast it acts when it is inhaled, which allows patients to easily determine the right dose for symptom relief. (Grinspoon)

Psychotherapy can be defined as a dialogue between conflicting emotions. In conventional practice, a therapist serves as guide toward understanding the conflict and resolving one's real desires. However, with the posture of tolerance and introspection that is the natural adjunct to Marijuana Therapy, the presence of an external guide is not needed and can actually be distracting. Serious desire to delve into one's own hidden agendas, with the enhanced awareness afforded by the Cannabis Sativa plant, can be a private, revelatory, restructuring of values, with another party only an intrusive element into the self-reflective consciousness. Self-medication with marijuana is actually a key to the much sought-after quietude that is the result of meditation. In the cases of PTSD, the slowing down of the frames of thought that occurs with the *marijuana consciousness* allows for the emergence of objective witnessing, thereby ameliorating the intense emotion of purely subjective experience.

While Marijuana Therapy can rebalance the dysfunctional amygdala from a physiological standpoint, residual psychological habitual fears are further de-energized through the "witnessing" aspect that attends the effects of marijuana. The ability to transcend one's personal agendas through the broadening perspective that accompanies the *marijuana consciousness* affords the emotional distance needed to heal the habit of fearfulness.

In keeping with the hopeful healing effects of marijuana for PTSD, the medical department of the Israeli army has funded a study with Hebrew University to examine the benefits of marijuana to treat PTSD for its combat soldiers.

THE SPIRITUAL COMPONENT

Many people who endure horrible experiences do not develop any long lasting emotional scars. For them, a deep, abiding trust in the forces of life may serve as an impenetrable protection against all assaults. For others, trust in everything may be demolished. For the person who develops PTSD, however, there is no returning to the innocence that existed prior to the traumatic "event." The sense of betrayal, guilt, and loss of meaning for the victim results in a personality forever changed.

Having one's belief system shaken to the core is the subjective experience that leads to PTSD. Everyone needs a "safe base" of normalcy. When one's comfort zone is violently and suddenly wrenched away, it can be interpreted by the victim as a rejection from everything one holds in the highest regard. Feeling abandoned by God; being utterly disillusioned with the atrocities inflicted by the human race; having the sense of oneself shattered; experiencing guilt, shame, mental confusion, and a sense of futility are the signposts of spiritual alienation. Unless the victim of PTSD can make sense out of the precipitating horrific incident(s), the indelible memory is persistent.

For some component of the PTSD population, the potential exists for transcending the damaged belief system, specifically because there is great motivation to end the suffering and also there exists an inordinate intensity of energy that can be re-channeled toward consciousness rather than away from it. Marijuana Therapy returns the organism to balance.

The continuous state of hyper-arousal, fear, and general confusion is eliminated as a result of the expansion in the breath. The energy level in the entire organism is raised, allowing for a higher perspective. Feelings of aloneness, lack of purpose, guilt and shame can be dissolved if one feels the connectedness of life. For some unknown portion of the PTSD population, intuition of a spiritual ground can precipitate a conversion to a deep non-attached acceptance of the trauma, whereby the memory becomes narrative without emotional content, because the perspective has switched from self-centered to all-centered.

Chapter 11 • Alzheimer's Disease
Progressive neurological degeneration caused by undernourishment of brain cells

To Breathe is To Live - Not To Breathe is To Die
To Breathe Partially over a Lifetime is To Die Slowly

Although Alzheimer's Disease (AD) occurs mostly in the elderly population, it is not a function of old age, but is instead a reflection of the health of the whole organism. Whenever there is imbalance, there is stress, accompanied by irregular and insufficient respiration which over time degrades into sickness. Nervousness, worry, striving and rushing are the hallmarks of daily living, with very little time set aside for healthy relaxation. Watching TV, phone conversations, computer distraction, music entertainment, restaurants, massage and tanning keeps just about every sense organ busy throughout the waking hours. Even if the body is still, the mind is busy. While the organism maintains constant activity, it is not surprising that 25% of the population wear out their brains long before the potential life-span.

After living with decreased oxygenation to the body for nearly decades, it is predictable that there is a lessening of brain-function. Alzheimer's Disease begins to be noticeable just about the 65th year of living. Malnourishment of neurons, involved in the complex electro/chemical connections in the brain over decades results in clumps of proteins being deposited in the arteries. Progressively increasing blockage is the result, which hampers the incredibly extensive and complicated network of communication between the cells. Thinking, talking and general behavior are all compromised in mirror image to what is happening to the weakened brain. Although scientific research has attempted to locate specific components and systems of abnormality that cause the brain degradation, the holistic explanation is simply that the whole organism has been damaged by the lack of breathing fully over so many years. Depending upon individual limitations, Alzheimer's Disease is often the first life-threatening manifestation of disease.

In 2737 BC - Emperor Shen Nung compiled the first Chinese Pharmacopoeia. Marijuana was classified as one of the Superior Elixirs of Immortality. It was prescribed for absent-mindedness.

Because Alzheimer's is so widespread, so feared, and so misunderstood, and also the fourth leading cause of death, an enormous body of scientific work has been conducted into the causes and treatments of this ever-increasing problem. At the present time, there are upwards of 4 million patients with Alzheimer's Disease in the U.S. By mid–century 14 million victims of Alzheimer's are predicted. That figure for the world-wide population estimate is 106 million victims.

The cannabinoids of Cannabis Sativa are Neuro-Protective and Anti-Inflammatory. Numerous studies on Alzheimer's Disease have examined the intricate chemical malfunctioning that takes place in the brain which causes the protein deposits (known as "plaques"), as well as investigating their exact composition. One of the specific facts that has come out of the investigations concerning Alzheimer's Disease is that the cannabinoid molecules of the marijuana plant actually intervene at one level of the complex chemical interactions within the brain to stop the dangerous build-up of plaques!

Neuro-Protective Effects of Cannabis

Over time, owing to the lack of oxygenation, cells in the brain slowly begin to die. Cannabinoids have been shown to stop the plaque-producing-combinations which cause blockage, thereby allowing for oxygen to flow through the arteries and capillaries to nourish the cells. Usually, natural brain-cannabinoids serve both anti-inflammatory and neuro-protective functions. However, the brains of Alzheimer's patients demonstrate less-than-normal working cannabinoid receptors, pointing to the undeniable fact, that the Cannabinoid System has not been working efficiently, resulting a loss of the proven neuro-protective effects of the cannabinoids.

Anti-Inflammatory Effects of Cannabis

Scientific studies tested the effects of THC in the laboratory and with animals. The results demonstrate that THC (from the Cannabis Sativa plant) inhibits the action of the enzyme, AChE (acetylcholinesterase). AChE is one of the known negative components in Alzheimer's Disease and helps to accelerate the plaque-formations. By administering the

THC, no binding of AChE to the proteins could occur and therefore no plaques were formed. Experiments found that THC actually disrupted the abnormal clumping of twisted proteins. In fact, THC could prevent AChE from forming plaques 100% of the time – as compared with prescribed drugs (with ratings of success ranging only from 7% to 22%) approved for use against Alzheimer's, all with life-threatening potential side-effect. THC, on the other hand is a natural, compatible, totally successful remedy.

Cognitive Decline Prevented with the Administration of Plant Cannabinoids

Animal Experimentation has demonstrated that plaques (already formed) which cause the cognitive decline in Alzheimer's Disease are actually neutralized with cannabinoids. Rats - injected with the plaque causing protein (amyloid) without also being given cannabinoids could not learn simple tasks. Rats that were given both the dreaded plaque-producing amyloid proteins in conjunction with the cannabinoids performed tasks as easily as the normal (untreated) group. Besides forming the blockages in arteries, amyloid proteins are responsible for inflammation which is a one of the well-known contributing factor to Alzheimer's. When marijuana cannabinoids were given, there was no inflammation!

"These findings - that cannabinoids work both to prevent inflammation and to protect the brain may set the stage for their use as a therapeutic approach for Alzheimer's disease." (de Ceballos, Cajai Insitute, Madrid). However, regardless of the intricacies of the electro/chemical/magnetic functioning within the brain - which according to research is dependent on efficient Cannabinoid Systemic operation - from a holistic standpoint, the fact that marijuana increases oxygenation to the entire body is of paramount importance. What transpires in the minute cellular world of the brain and which is only visible under the microscope hinges on the health of the entire organism which is evidenced in the pattern of the breath.

The normal adult human brain has at least 11 billion neurons. Connections to other brain cells have been estimated at the incredible number of between 5 and 10 quadrillion, depending on age (children have the highest), so that each neuron can receive input from some

10,000 – 20,000 other neurons. Receiving, processing and relaying messages determines our perceptions, actions, emotions and thoughts, all of which takes an enormous amount of energy. Even though the brain only weighs only a few pounds, it needs a full 20% of the body's oxygen supply.

Marijuana Therapy is the most direct and most sensible method for retaining full oxygenation of the organism under times of stress, when the breathing is most taxed.

There is nothing mysterious about Alzheimer's Disease. It is simply impossible for the oxygenated blood to circulate properly to the brain cells because of blockage. It is hindered from free flow and therefore is unable to nourish the quadrillions of interconnections among neurons sufficiently. In addition, the circulating blood, itself is not adequately oxygenated owing to the long-term contractive habit of the breath.

Acute Blockage in the Circulatory System to the Brain Causes Stroke.

Chronic Diminishment in the Circulatory System to the Brain Results in Alzheimer's Disease.

The health of the heart which pumps the oxygenated blood (from the lungs) to the brain is a very significant feature in determining the potential for Alzheimer's Disease. With every heartbeat, 25% of the organism's blood supply is sent to the brain. Damage or dysfunction in any part of the Circulatory or Respiratory System, such as coronary disease, a prior stroke, diabetes, high blood pressure, high cholesterol and of course, diminished lung capacity, increase the risk of developing Alzheimer's Disease. These illnesses all point to the common element among the risk factors as lack of oxygen. In fact, over the last few years, research into the lack of sufficient oxygen has recognized it as the root cause of the plaques which clog the arteries in the brain. According to Weihong Song from the University of BC in Vancouver, "vasodilators, which enlarge the blood vessels, may help," - which is one of the main effects of Marijuana Therapy.

Investigation into other risk factors have concluded that heavy snorers have a higher risk of developing Alzheimer's disease, due to lack of oxygen.

Since the link between hypoxia (O2 deficiency from impaired blood flow) and Alzheimer's Disease has been established, further research is being conducted into the connections between coronary disease and Alzheimer's since the afflictions of the heart and brain share the common problems of inflammation, oxidative stress, and hypoxia.

Marijuana Therapy is anti-oxidant, anti-inflammatory, increases the oxygen carrying ability of the blood vessels as well as increasing the oxygen being transported.

In addition to studying how the health of the heart affects the health of the brain, science is also examining the relationship between Diabetes and Alzheimer's. According to the latest scientific opinion, blood sugar elevation (the signature of Diabetes), may damage the cells by accumulating in the brain. Patients with high blood sugar, yet still in a pre-Diabetic classification, have an increased risk of 70% of developing dementia and /or Alzheimer's Disease. In patients with high blood pressure, there was an even greater risk.

Marijuana Therapy Lowers Blood Sugar and Helps to Control Blood Sugar Levels in Diabetes.

Marijuana Therapy Lowers Blood Pressure.

Alzheimer's Disease – The Shrinking Brain

In the early stages of Alzheimer's Disease, the Hippocampus part of the brain is one of the first regions to suffer damage. Forgetfulness, the inability to form new memories and disorientation are among the first symptoms. The hippocampus is especially sensitive to global reductions in oxygen levels in the body, so that in periods of hypoxia, such as during a heart attack or in cases of almost drowning, "brain damage" to the hippocampus results. As the degeneration progresses, the brain matter shrinks, while the spaces between the cells enlarge. Symptoms worsen to where the victims of Alzheimer's Disease lose the ability to recognize familiar places and objects. Disorientation is common, along with agitation, loss of appetite, insomnia and the inability to speak.

Neurogenesis: The Growing Brain

"Neuro-genesis" is the birth of neurons. The human brain keeps on growing contrary to the long-held scientific hypothesis that brain cells were irreplaceable and determined at birth. In fact, research has demonstrated that throughout adult life, neurogenesis is ongoing. Preliminary research suggests that new brain-cell-creation in the adult hippocampus is needed to be able to form new associations as well as being able to recall the past. In addition, adult-born neurons have more excitability than older neurons, and appear to play a role in how the organism handles stress. In adults who suffer from lack of sleep, there is a marked reduction of neurogenesis in the hippocampus. Chronic stress, aging, and depression are also responsible for decrease in the process of neurogenesis. By contrast, healthy life-styles, especially aerobic exercise, a forward looking attitude, as well as varied experiences, even intellectually-taxing jobs all play their part in encouraging neurogenesis.

Neurogenesis Sparked by Synthetic Marijuana

According to a study conducted at the University of Saskatchewan (Xia Zhang researcher), the stereo-typical notion that marijuana kills brain cells and/or damages the brain is completely incorrect. The cells of the hippocampus nearly all demonstrate the presence of the CB1 cannabinoid receptor. In a scientific experiment, by administering a concentrated synthetic cannabinoid into the brains of rats, noticeable, increased neurogenesis occurred in the hippocampus within ten days.

During that time, the dosed rats were less anxious and not as depressed, which pointed to the anti-stress effects of having an expanded brain (attendant to increased oxygenation). The scientific study agrees with the human subjective experience of marijuana and with the holistic observation of increased health with regular employment of marijuana, and includes the ancient appreciation of the adaptogenic quality of the Cannabis plant.

Modern science has validated what was empirically, intuitively, and observably clear: Marijuana Therapy helps the brain to operate more efficiently.

When examining the advantages of Marijuana Therapy for Alzheimer's Disease, it is the whole plant that is being discussed, with emphasis on the leaves and flowers, for they are the classic definition of "marijuana." Whether Cannabis is eaten, vaporized, smoked, drunk or in any medical or novel way incorporated into the human body, its benefits are monumental for health. Its specific remedial applications appear as limitless as the number of problems that can occur in the integrity of the organism, at all levels. Since this article is specific to Alzheimer's Disease, it is absolutely essential that the oil obtained from the seeds of Cannabis Sativa/Hemp also be included in this discussion.

Benefits of Hemp Seed Oil

The fact that Hemp seed has been consumed by mankind (and animals) for thousands of years has been lost to modern civilization even though, historically, entire populations survived with only hemp seed in times of famine. The fruit of the Cannabis Sativa plant is unique in its nutritional bounty. Hemp Seed is a super food from nature with three nutritional wonders: 1) Hemp seed has a perfect balance of Omega 3 and Omega 6 fatty acids - essential for heart / brain health; 2) Hemp seed has a full amino acid spectrum – that is, it is a complete protein; and 3) Hemp seed has an abundance of trace minerals, many of which are beneficial to health.

For the progressive degeneration caused by Alzheimer's Disease, the constituents of Hemp Seed is a necessity. It is a known fact that populations in countries with a high intake of fish from the sea suffer far less incidence of brain degeneration, specifically because of their Omega fatty acid content. New research demonstrates that high amounts of one of the omega-3 fatty acids docosahexaenoic acid, or DHA -- may protect against the memory loss caused by Alzheimer's, even when there are already brain lesions indicating advanced disease. The researchers speculate that DHA may prevent or slow Alzheimer's progression by protecting against damage to the area where brain cells communicate. Damage to these "synaptic" areas is known to impair memory and learning ability and typically occurs in Alzheimer's patients. In fact, several studies have demonstrated that people who regularly have high intake of DHA in Omega-3 Fatty Acids have a lower risk of developing Alzheimer's Disease.

Hemp Oil is comprised of 75-90% Essential Fatty Acids, with all the Omegas (3-6-9) as well as the rare GLA (GammoLineic Acid). The "Essential" classification is simply because the human body needs them for complete health but cannot produce them. Essential Fatty Acids have been shown as preventive in artery clogging and heart disease because it lowers cholesterol and encourages weight loss. Hemp oil is full of Vitamins B1, B2, B6 and E (an antioxidant).

Palliation of Symptoms with Marijuana Therapy

As Alzheimer's Disease progresses, symptoms become worse: Mental confusion, anger, agitation, insomnia, loss of appetite, pessimism and depression become prevalent. Prescribed drugs are admittedly inadequate at best and at worst, severely harmful to the elderly patient, whose system is too fragile for many of the drugs.

Marijuana Therapy can help:

Although great strides have been made in recent studies that give insight into the mechanism of the disease process, Alzheimer's is still officially considered of unknown origin, irreversible and fatal. Holistic Health on the other hand views Alzheimer's Disease as the predictable result of poor lifestyle, which includes diet, physical and mental behavior and environmental factors. Individual tendencies and weaknesses of the patient are considered aides toward custom-tailored habits of health, rather than prognosticators of predetermined inherited disease. Although in the later stages, after organic deterioration has occurred, the prognosis for the Alzheimer's patient is poor, nevertheless, the evidence suggests that taking precautionary and pro-active measures before the disease is fully entrenched, in fact, does ameliorate the symptoms as well as lessening the advance of the degeneration.

Marijuana Therapy is in the first line of defense, which in this case, includes the addition of Omega 3 & Omega 6 Fatty Acids (safely obtained from Hemp Seed Oil without any contamination as with fish), as well as the elimination of unhealthy habits of living. Later on with progressive deterioration in the functioning of the brain, sleep disturbances, delusions, pacing, compulsive movements, and even abusive, threatening language to caregivers is seen. Here again: Certain Compounds of Cannabis Sativa Alleviate the Symptoms of Alzheimer's

Disease.

Different compounds in Cannabis Sativa have specific actions that are especially beneficial for the Alzheimer's patient. Cannabidiol (CBD) works mostly to protect brain cells from atrophy and direct damage owing to malnourishment and miscommunication. The research clearly indicates that there is less blockage of arteries owing to the presence of CBD. The oil from the seeds of the plant - full of Omega 3 & 6 "essential" Fatty Acids, and a multitude of vitamins - serves as superior food for the cells in their ability to thrive.

The Molecule of Psychological Enhancement

The other common cannabinoid from the plant, the famous THC, has beneficial results for the general agitation so common in the later stages of Alzheimer's. Relaxation of the musculature, oxygenation of the hypoxic cells of the brain (and the rest of the body) and balance of the ANS have noticeable toning down effects to generalized nervous energy seen in over 75% of patients. In addition to calming the agitated Alzheimer's patient, and lifting the mood from pessimism to optimism, the "munchies" of Cannabis is a wonderfully beneficial side-effect. All these positive additional benefits of Marijuana Therapy happen quite simultaneously. Breath is deepened and slowed, mental confusion is moderated to a more relaxed thinking, and the anorexic Alzheimer's patient becomes hungry!

So often, in the later stages of the disease, a "wasting syndrome" occurs owing to a complete distaste for all food. One of the most well-known and documented effects of Marijuana Therapy is its appetite-stimulating actions. Not only does the patient become in the mood to enjoy nourishment, the digestive process is likewise improved with the administration of marijuana. There is no doubt that Marijuana Therapy improves the quality of life for the person with Alzheimer's Disease: calmer, hungrier and happier translates into the appropriate treatment modality for anyone.

Cannabis Sativa is a plant that predates human history which means it was around before people. As far back as researchers can trace the activities of human beings, Cannabis was there as constant companion. As a health giving herb, as a specific remedy for sickness, for raising the spirit and appreciating the wonder of existence, this plant is/was revered world-wide. Generally speaking, throughout all of this long and wonderful association with the human race, marijuana was not smoked as a cigarette. It was drunk or eaten or it was inhaled as pure smoke with no addition of processed paper. For the elderly patient, the method of administration of Marijuana Therapy, most often considered is - a pastry, a cup of tea, a capsule of Cannabis butter, and the pure vaporized cannabinoids.

To ameliorate the agitation that overwhelms many patients at the end of the day (known as *sundowner's syndrome*) – an afternoon cup of Cannabis tea has been reported by many of the caretakers of Alzheimer's patients as very beneficial. It is during the late afternoon and early evening that the patient becomes fidgety, may pace without purpose for hours, has no appetite because of confused restlessness, and may even become abusive in language and gesture.

Marijuana Therapy ends the agitation, stops the pacing, increases the appetite and oftentimes allows the patient to center his/her thoughts. According to one caregiver, "She would become more pleasant, less aggressive. The pacing, fidgeting, the agitation left or subsided....She would be able to sit down and enjoy a TV program. The tea would work great." No doubt, the calming yet simultaneous energizing effects of THC improve the patient's quality of life. The experience of "being high" is not lost on the person with Alzheimer's Disease.

Not being able to sleep or not being able to sleep a full night often plagues the Alzheimer's *patient* and the *caregiver*. There are numerous anecdotal reports of how the sedative effects of marijuana help, first to calm the agitation, and then to allow the person to drift off into a peaceful and full night of sleep. Although studies have yet to be conducted concerning insomnia and the benefits of Marijuana Therapy, there is no doubt that future research will validate the efficient, healthful, non-addicting, safe Cannabis Sativa plant as a superior method for overcoming insomnia. These future results will validate what the legendary Emperor Shen Nung knew back in 2737 BC when he prescribed the Cannabis plant for insomnia. From ancient times, Indian Bhang was known to induce sleep. In pre-modern Japan, marijuana was used as a safe natural medicine for insomnia. The 1937 U.S. Pharmacopoeia prescribed Cannabis for its sedative qualities.

Marijuana Therapy to Alleviate Stress of the Caregiver

Alzheimer's Disease is often said to have two victims: the patient and the caregiver who is witnessing the deterioration of a loved one (often a spouse or parent) as a personal, life-altering loss, while also being in charge of the daily hassles, simultaneously caring for the worsening state of the patient. The extreme (sometimes killing) stressors of the caregiver range from financial worry to emotional isolation, and include dealing with the patient's disorientation, physical disabilities, rage, insomnia and wanderings. Surely Marijuana Therapy is indicated for such a broad spectrum of physical and psychological disruptions. Benefits from the stress-relieving qualities of marijuana, suggest that a more conscious and accepting attitude of both suffering and death can be attained, which will be seen in a calmer, more loving, more competent and less worried attitude about the future inevitability.

Works of Interest

Bloomquist, E.R., 1968, Marijuana: Social Benefit or Social Detriment; Glencoe Press, MN.

Browbill. C.J., 1979, "He encourages dagga smoking for African mine workers," Thesis, Edinburgh University, London.

Carstairs, G.M., 1954, "Daru and Bhang: Cultural Factors in the Choices of Intoxicants," J. of Study of Alcohol, 15:220-237.

Chernin, M., 1981, Health: Holistic Approach, Theosophical Publishing.

Clarke, R.C., 1977, Botany & Ecology of Cannabis, PODS Press, CA.

Creighton, C., 1903. "On Indication: the Hasheesh Vice in The Old Testament," Janus, 8:301, 243-246, 297-301, Amsterdam.

Dorabush. et al., 1977, Chronic Cannabis, Annals of Acad. of Science.

Fairchild, Jordon and Fairchild, Mickey, 1971, "Quantitative Analysis of Some Drug Effects on EEG by Long Term Frequency Analysis, "Proceedings of the Western Pharmacology Society, 14:135-140.

Fishel, Ruth, 1991, The Healing Energy, Health Communications, Deerfield Beach, FL.

Graham, J.D.P., 1976, Cannabis and Health, Academic Press, London.

Kabelik, et al., 1959, "Hemp: An Antibiotic," Pharmazie, 14: 349-355

Ludlow, F.H.. 1857, "The Hasheesh Eater: being Passages from Life of a Pythagorean," Harper Bros, NY.

Novak, William, 1980, High Culture, .Alfred Knopft & Co., NY.

Pliny, 1938, Natural History, (ed. H. Rachman), BOOK, XIX: 5

Rosenthal, F., 1971, The Herb: Hasheesh In Medieval Muslim Society, Leiden Press, London.

Rubin, V. et al, 1975, "Ganja in Jamaica, Mouton. The Hague. Sastn, Solomon, D. 1972, The Marijuana Papers, New Amer.Lib., N.Y. Souif, MJ., 1966. "Hasheesh Consumption (Egypt)," Hunter, London.

Walton, R., 1938. "Marijuana: America - Drug Problem: Mexicans Work Better with Marijuana; W. B. Saunder & Co.,

Weber, F., 1971, Drug Beat, McGraw-Hill, NY

Wilkinson, 1929, "Cannabis/Indica: Historical Pharmacological Study of the Drug," British J. of Inebriety.

Bibliography

Abel, Ernest L. M., 1977, The First 12,000 Years, Plenum Press, NY.

Abramov, Aya et al., 1995, "An Efficient New Cannabinoid Anti-emetic in Pediatric Oncology," Life Sciences, vol. 56, No. 23/24: 2097-2102.

Abrams, Donald, 1995, "U.S. Stalls over tests of marijuana to treat AIDS Patients," Nature, Vol. 374.

Ajaya, Swami, Ph.D., 1977, Foundations of Eastern and Western Psychology, Himalayan Institute Press, Glenview, IL.

Ajaya, Swami, Ph.D., 1983, Psychotherapy: East and West, Himalayan Institute Press, Honesdale, PA.

Albright. Peter, M.D., 1980, Body, Mind and Spirit, The Stephen Greene Press, Brattleboro, VT.

Auld, John, 1981, Marijuana Use and Social Control, Academic Press, London.

Bates, Charles, 1986, Ransoming the Mind, Yes International Pub., St. Paul, MN.

Becker, B.S., 1963, Outsiders: Studies in the Sociology of Deviance, Macmillan, NY.

Benson, Herbert, M.S., 1975, The Relaxation Response, William Morrow and Co.. NY.

Bodson, H.L. et al., 1981, "Cannabis and Nausea," J. Clinical Pharmacology, 21, 235-295.

Brecher, Ed., M.Ed., 1969, Licit and Illicit Drugs, Little Brown, Boston.

Canon, Walter, 1932, The Wisdom of the Body, W.W. Norton and Co., N.Y.

Capra, Fritjof, 1988, "The New Physics: Implications for Psych." The American Theosophist. 68, No.5 (May 1980): 114, 116.

Carter, William E., 1980, "Cannabis in Costa Rica: A Study of Chronic Marijuana Use," Institute for the Study of Human Issues, Philadelphia. Caswell. A., 1992, "Marijuana as Medicine," Medical Journal of Australia. Vol. J: l56.

Chopra and Chopra, 1957, "The Use of Cannabis Drugs in India," Bulletin of Narcotics, 9:13.

Chopra, and Chopra, 1939. "The Present Position of Hemp Drug Addiction in India," Indian Med. Research, M. 3.1-1-19.

Chisti, Hakim, G.M., 1988, The Traditional Healer, Healing Arts Press, Rochester, VT.

Cluss and Firemean, 1985, "Recent Trends in Asthma Research," Annals of Behavioral Medicine, 7(4), 11-16 (238).

Cohen, Sidney, 1975, Marijuana Alert, UCLA Project, Station KNBC

Conrad, C. 1993, Lifeline to the Future, Creative Xpressions, CA Creer,

T..L., 1988, "The Synthesis of Medical and Behavioral Sciences with Respect to Bronchial Asthma." Erlbaum, N.J.

Dastur. J.F., F.N.I., 1962, Medicinal Plants of India and Pakistan, D.B. Tavaporevala Sons & Co., Private Ltd., Bombay, India.

Deikman, A.J., 1971, "Bimodal Consciousness," Archives of General Psychiatry, 25:481-89.

Devane, W.A, et at, 1992, "Anandamide and Extra-pyramidal Function," Science, Vol. 56, No. 23/24,258,1946-1949.

Devane, W.A., et al, 1987. " Cannabinoid Analgesic Inhibit Neuronal Adenylate Cyclase and Bind to Brain Receptor," St. Louis School of Medicine, St. Louis, MO.

1992. "Isolation & Structure of Brain Constituent that Bonds to Cannabinoid Receptor," Science. 258: 1946-1949

1993. Cannabis: The Brain's Other Supplier, New Scientist, Vol. 31. "Enzymatic Synthesis of Anandamide" Laboratory of Biology NIMA, Bethseda, MD.

Di Marzo, Vincenzo, 2004, Instituto per la Chimica di Molecole di Interesse Biologico - CNR

Doblin & Klemman, 1991, "Marijuana as Anti-emetic Medicine: A Survey of Oncologists," J. of Clinical Oncology, vol. 9, 1314-1319.

Dreher, M. et al., "Prenatal Marijuana Exposure and Neonatal Outcomes in Jamaica: Ethnographic Study, "Pediatrics, Vol. 93, #2, '94

Dwarkanath, C., 1965, "The Uses of Opium and Cannabis in Systems of Medicine in India," Bulletin of Narcotic, 17:15-19.

Dychtwald, Ken, 1977, Body-Mind, Jeremy Tarcher. LA. CA

Einstein, A., 1954. Einstein: Ideas and Opinions, Crown Press. NY.

Ferguson, Marilyn, 1973, The Brain Revolution, Bantam Books. NY.

Fishkin. S. et al., 1978, "Drugs and Consciousness," (Sugarman and Tarter).

Flom, F. et al., 1975, "Marijuana smoking reduced pressure in human eyes" Invest. Ophthalmology, 14:52.

French-Constant, C., 1994, "Pathogenesis of M.S.,"The Lancet, Vol. 343

Freund-Levi, Yvonne, et al., 2006, "Omega-3 oils & marijuana may stave off Alzheimer's" Karolinska Institute, Sweden.

Getman, John, "Marijuana and the Human Brain," High Times, 3/95.

Ginsberg, A., 1966, "The Great Marijuana Hoax: First Manifesto to End the Bring down," Atlantic Monthly, November: 104, 107-112.

Gorman, Peter, "Ralph Seeley, Fighting for Life," High Times, 2/96.

Gray, Jeffrey, 1971, The Psychology of Fear and Stress, McGraw Hill.

Grinspoon, Lester, M.D., 1971, Marijuana Reconsidered, Quick Pub.

Grinspoon & Bakalar, 1993, Marihuana, The Forbidden Medicine, Yale University, New Haven and London.

Grinspoon & Bakalar, 1995, "Marijuana as Medicine": A Plea for Reconsideration, JAMA, June 21, Vol. 273.p. 1875-1876.

Green, Keith, et al., 1976, "Editorials on Recent Advances," Invest. Ophthalmology, 14:261

Green, Keith, et al., 1978 "Cannabinoid effects on the eye," Ex. .Res., 24:189-96.

Green, Keith, et al., 1979 "Interaction of adrenergic antagonists with prostaglandin E and Tetrahydrocannabinol in eyes," Invest.. Ophth:15:102

Green, Keith, et al., 1977, "Mediation of ocular tetrohydrocannabinol effects by adrenergic nervous system," Exp. Eye Res., 25:119-140. Green, Keith, et al., 1976, "Effect of tetrahydrocannabinol on aqueous dynamics in rabbit," Exp. Eye Res., 15:499-507. Green, Keith, et al., "Aqueous humor formation," Exp. Eye Res, 26:65-69.

Grof, Stanislov, M.D:, 1988, The Adventure of Self-Discovery, SUNY Press, Albany, NY.

Grotenhermen, F. Kann, 2002, "Can Cannabis be used in an arising panic attack?", Hanf-Magazin

Gunderson, Carl H., "The impact of new pharmaceutical agents on the cost of neurological care," J. of Neur., Mar., '95:45.

Guzman, M., et al., 2001, "Control of the cell survival/death decision by cannabinoids." J. Mol Med 78(11): 613-25.

Halikas, et al., 1971, "Marijuana Effects: A Survey of Regular Users," JAMA, 217:1392.

Herer, Jack, 1985, "Hemp & The Marijuana Conspiracy: The Emperor Wears No Clothes," HEMP Publishing, Van Nuys CA.

Helper, et al., 1971. "Marijuana Smoking and Intro ocular Pressure," JAMA, 217:1392.

Hockman, J. 1972, Marijuana and Social Evolution, Prentice Hall, NY.
    1990, "Cannabinoid Actions," St. Louis Univ., St. Louis, MO.
Howlett, A., 1987, "Regulation of Adenylate Cyclase in Cultured
    Neuronal Cell Line" by Marijuana Constituents, St. Louis Univ.
    MO., 1990, "Metabolites of Delta-9 and Synthetic Analogs with
    Psycho-activity," St. Louis Univ. MO.
Indian Hemp Drugs Commission, 1969, "Marijuana: Report of 1893-
    1894," Waverly Press, MD
Inglis, 1975, "The Forbidden Game," Charles Scribners & Sons, N.Y.
Iversen, Leslie, 1993, "Medical Uses of Marijuana," Nature;V/375.
Joy, JE, Watson, SJ, & Benson, JA, eds., 1999, Marijuana and medicine:
    Assessing the science base. Institute of Medicine. Washington,
    DC. National Academy Press
Jung, C.G., 1986, Collected Works of C. G. Jung, , R.F.C. Hull (trans.),
    Bollingen Series, No. 20, Princeton Univ. Press., Princeton, NJ.
Krishnamurti, J., 1971, The Flight of the Eagle, Harper and Row, NY.
Kuechenmeister, et al., 1975, "Marijuana, Heart Rate, EEG Response,"
    Research Communications on Chemical Pathology, 10:201-211.
Kupersmith, MJ., 1994, "Mega-dose Corticosteroid in Multiple
    Sclerosis," Neurology, January.
Kusher, David, I., 1994, "Effect of the Psychoactive Metabolite of
    Marijuana, on Synthesis of Tumor Necrosis Factor by Human
    Large Granular Lymphocytes," Cellular Immunology: 154.
Lad, Vasant, 1986, "The Yoga of Herbs," Ayurvedic Wellness Journal.
    Life Sciences, Vol. 56, No. 23/24: 2097-2107.
Lowen, A., 1970, Pleasure, Penguin Books, Ltd., Harmondsworth,
    England.
Margolis, et al., 1970, "A Child's Garden of Grass," Pocket Books, NY.
Marsicano, G. et al., 2002 "The endogenous cannabinoid system controls
    extinction of aversive memories." Nature, 418, 530-534
Maslow, Abraham, 1968, Toward a Psychology of Being, Van Nostrand
    Rienhold, NY.
Maslow, Abraham, 1971, The Further Reaches of Human Nature, Viking
Mathew, Roy, 1989, "Acute Changes in Cerebral Blood Flow After
    Smoking Marijuana," Life Sciences, Vol. 52.
Mayor LaGuardia's Committee on Marijuana, 1994, "The Marijuana
    Problem in the City of New York," Jaques Cattell Press,
    Lancaster, PA.
McKenna, Terrence, 1992, Food of the Gods, Bantam Books, NY.

Mechoulam, Ralph, 1990, "Cannabinoids as Therapeutic Agents," CRC Press, Boca Raton, FL.

Melnck, H.M., 1989, "Effect of Cannabinoids on Spasticity and Ataxia in Multiple Sclerosis," JN, Vol. 235.

Merlin, Mark D., 1972, Man and Marijuana, Assoc. Univ. Press, N.Y.

Merritt, J. et al., "Effect of Marijuana on Intraocular and Blood Pressure in Glaucoma," Presented: 84th Meeting of American Academy of Ophth., San Francisco

Mestel, R., 1993, "Cannabis: The Brain's Other Supplier," New Scientist. July 31

Mikurlya, Tod, 1970, "Marijuana Medical Papers," The Medical Times, 98:187-191.

Morgan, John, M.D., 1992, "Drugs in America," Speech delivered at PA State Univ., January 29.

Munro, Sean, 1993, "Molecular characterization of a peripheral receptor for cannabinoids," Nature; Vol. 365.

National Organization For the Reform of Marijuana Laws (NORML), 1995, Activist Packet. Washington, DC.

New York Times, 1996. "AMA Shelves Disputed Report on Drugs," June 23

Ornstein. R. and Sobel, G., 1990. "The Healing Brain." Guilford Press, NY.

Pelletier, Kenneth R., 1977, *Mind as Heater, Mind as Slayer,* Merloyd Lawrence Books, NY. *-1981, Longevity,* Merloyd Lawrence Books, NY. - and Garfield, Charles, 1976, *Consciousness: East and West,* Harper-Colophon Books, Harper and Row, NY.

Prakesh, Om, 1961, *Food and Drink .in Ancient India,* Munshi Ram, Monohar LAL, Delhi.

Prince, G., 1978, "Putting the Other Half of the Brain to Work," *Training: The Magazine of Human Resources Development,* 15:57.

Rama, Swami, Ballantine, Rudolph, M.D.• Ajaya, Swami, 1976, *Yoga and Psychotherapy,* Himalayan Inst., Honesdale, PA.

Rama, Swami, Ballantine, RUdolph, M.D., Hymes, Alan, MD, 1979. *Science of Breath,* Himalayan Inst. Press, Honesdale, PA.

Rosenberg, Jack Lee; and Rand, Marjorie L., 1985. *Body Self and Soul,* Humanics, Ltd., Atlanta, GA.

Ruddock, E. Harris, M.D., 1974. Text Book of Modern Medicine and Surgery on Homeopathic Principles, Homeopathic Publishing

Co., London.

Sagan, Carl, 1977, *Dragons of Eden,* Random House, NY.

Samkara, Sri, *Thou Art That,* Upadesa Sahasrl, Verse 209, Chapler 18, New Delhi.

Saraswati, Swami Satyananda. 1984, *Kundalini Tantra,* Munzar, Bihar, India.

Schaef, Anne Wilson 1987, *When Society Becomes An Addict,* Harper and Row, San Francisco.

Science Daily, 2005, *Journal of Neuroscience* "synthetic analogue of the active component of marijuana may reduce the inflammation and prevent the mental decline associated with Alzheimer's disease". Cajal Institute & Complutense University, Madrid

Seeley, Ralph, "1996 High Times" Article, Feb.

Secretary of Health and Human Services, 1974: "Marijuana and Health." Fourth Annual Report to the U.S. Congress & 1980, Eighth Annual Report to the U.S. Congress.

Shultes, Richard Evans and Hofman, Albert, 1993, Plants of the Gods, Inner Traditions, NY.

Snyder, S.H., 1972, Uses of Marijuana, Oxford Press, NY.

Springer, Sally P. and Deutsch, George, W,H.. 1981, Left Brain, Right Brain, W. H. Freeman and Co.. NY.

Sugerman, A. and Tarter, R., 1978, Expanding Dimensions of Consciousness, Springer Publishing, NY.

Stafford, P.G. and Golightly, B.H., 1967, LSD: The Problem Solving Psychedelic, Harper and Row, NY.

Tart, C., 1975, States of Consciousness, E.P. Dutton, NY.

Tashkin et at, 1973, "Acute Pulmonary Physiologic Effects of Smoked Marijuana and Oral Delta Tetrahydrocannabinoids in Healthy Young Men," N.E. *Journal of Medicine;* and 1975,"Effects of Smoked Marijuana in Experimentally Induced Asthma," *Amer. Rev. of Respiratory Disease.*

Van Dusen 1975, "LSD and the Enlightenment of Zen," Mendocino State Hospital Study, CA.

Weil, A., 1990, Natural Health, Natural Medicine, Houghton Mifflin Co., Boston.

Vaughn & Walsh, 1977, "The Transpersonal Perspective," Beyond Ego, (edit. C. Tart) Shambhala Publications, Boston.

Wallace, A., 1989, "Systems Science: Healing and Wellness," UMI Dissertation Information Services, Ann Arbor, MI.

Weil, A., 1980, "The Marriage of the Sun and The Moon," Houghton Mifflin, Boston.

Weil, A. et al., 1983, Chocolate to Morphine, Houghton Mifflin Co., Boston.

Weizman, F., 1993, "Anandamide," Institute of Science in Rehovot, Israel, Scientist, vol. 7, No. 14, July 12.

White. John, ed., 1977, "Kundalini Evolution and Enlightenment," Anchor Press/Doubleday, Garden City, NJ.

Wilbur, Ken, 1985, "No Boundary," Shambhala, Boston and London.

Wooton Committee Report, 1968, "Marihuana," London.

Yuasa, Yasuo, 1987, "The Body," SUNY Press, Albany.

Zlas, Jo et al., 1993, "Early Medical Use of Cannabis," Nature, vol. 363, May.

THE PEOPLE'S CLASS ACTION LAWSUIT:

At the time that this law suit was launched, marijuana was barely recognized by the authorities as having any medicinal qualities. Going public with the need and employment of Cannabis for relief of suffering and for the natural birthright to minister to one's own body was actually dangerous. The Drug War was in full force, and many patients were being arrested and imprisoned. The patients of the Class Action Lawsuit were pioneers in courage. Many of them were gravely ill. Many of them have since died. Their determination to have marijuana recognized as medicine, however, was not in vain. Their legacy is that the knowledge of the benefits of marijuana is growing exponentially every day. Citizens from all over the world are demanding governmental acknowledgement and sanction of medicinal marijuana. Laws are changing as are mainstream attitudes. However, patients are still being imprisoned, while progress in recognizing marijuana as a holy sacrament is only in its infancy.

"I am extremely gratified in the progress that we have made in putting together what we feel is one of the most important cases in the history of the United States. Petitioners-for-Plaintiff-Status now number more than five hundred and come from every state in the union. They share the common issue of being candidates for free and legal use of therapeutic Cannabis for their health, wellness, and quality of life."

This has been an enormous undertaking that has been carried entirely by Hirsch & Caplan Public Interest Law Firm. Special thanks to Joan Bello, Kay Lee, Michael Long and Ryan Perlman, whose dedication and hard work have been essential to our progress."

Peace, Love and Victory for the People
Lawrence Elliott Hirsch, Hirsch & Caplan Public Interest Law Firm

The People's Class Action Lawsuit for Freedom
From Government Prohibition of Therapeutic Cannabis
Filed on July 3, 1998
United States District Court
Eastern District of Pennsylvania, Philadelphia

Mar 3, 1999 First Public Hearing (75 of 165 plaintiffs attended.)
Dec. 1, 1999 Judge Marvin Katz dismissed the Lawsuit
May 10, 2000 Lead Plaintiff, Kiyoshi Kuromiya died

APPENDIX I – Patient Testimonials for Cannabis Therapeutics

Carlos A. (Colorado) is 52. In 1973 an auto accident left him a quadriplegic. Carlos also suffers from extremely high blood pressure. Doctors support his use of Cannabis, as it lowers his dangerous pressure in seconds, which nothing else does. "I am sure that without it, I would not be alive to give this testimony."

Jonathan A. (Hawaii) is 45 and has suffered from severe asthma since he was ten. He had to take "a steady schedule of twelve injections per day for over-production of histamines." When he became 18 he refused the injections. From then until the present, Jon has used only Cannabis for his health problems.

Bill A. (Michigan) is 40. He suffers from severe, post-traumatic headaches that are not relieved by conventional medications. He has no memory of his life before the accident, in which he was struck by a drunk driver. After seeing many specialists and trying countless medications, Bill has found that only Cannabis effectively releases him from his agony.

Lynn A. (Vermont) is 49. She has chronic-pain from sciatic nerve damage. After taking many prescribed drugs, Lynn began using Cannabis to avoid the addictive and debilitating side effects of conventional medications.

Hans A. (Ohio) is 29. He is HIV-positive and suffers from migraines due to an arachnoid cyst in the brain. He has been employing Cannabis to stimulate his appetite and reduce the pain of his headaches without taking prescription drugs.

Daniel A. (Ohio) is 41 and he is quadriplegic. Medication prescribed for his condition caused brain seizures. He has removed himself from all other medication and uses Cannabis to reduce spasms. "It also relieves my stress and suffering from a mental standpoint."

Tim B. (West Virginia) is 34. He underwent five operations following an automobile accident and was in the hospital for two years. He lost over half his body weight, received a new aorta made from gortex and had two cerebral strokes. He uses Cannabis because it is the only medicine that controls spasticity and allows him to eat and to sleep.

Robert B. (Texas) is 49. He was in a scooter accident in 1984 in which his leg was severely injured. After twenty-six operations, the leg was amputated. He was prescribed morphine, and strong hallucinogenic tranquilizers like Halcion. "Cannabis helps me to sleep; the throbbing in my stump is lessened and I can eat and maintain my weight."

MJ B. (Nebraska) is 48. She is the victim of a spinal cord injury and suffers from epilepsy. She has found Cannabis to be more effective and safer than other conventional medications. She began to self-medicate with the herb after opiate-type medications caused traumatic side effects.

William B (South Dakota) is 46. He has AIDS. His aggressive medication causes extreme fatigue, diarrhea, sporadic nausea, headaches, chronic skin rashes, nervousness, and loss of appetite. With the help of Cannabis, William relieves his headaches, reduces his nausea, and regains his appetite and energy level. He hopes it will be legal before he dies.

Trent B. (Utah) is 36. He suffers from ALS and is completely immobilized. He utilizes Cannabis because his esophagus is paralyzed. He cannot swallow without it. "I also use Cannabis for depression and to reduce pain."

Mark B (Connecticut) is 45 and is a paraplegic due to a fractured spine. Without the use of his lower body, he suffers from muscle spasms. He relies solely on a vegetable diet and Cannabis for pain and spasms.

Carey B. (Georgia) is 37. He is a quadriplegic who has multiple back and neck injuries. He uses Cannabis for the muscle spasms that conventional medication cannot relieve.

Frank B. (Vermont) is 48 and injured his back in the military. Doctors prescribed huge amounts of morphine that left him in· a "constant stupor." "Cannabis is my best medicine... It also reduces my level of anxiety."

Patricia C. (Florida) was diagnosed with bipolar disorder, arthritis, a neck injury, and tardive dyslexia. She utilizes Cannabis for stress, sleep, to reduce pain, and for muscle spasms.

Georgia C. (Vermont) is 50 and suffers from chronic pain and intestinal problems. Confined to a wheelchair, she needs Cannabis to alleviate pain, to relax her muscles, and reduce depression.

Alan Carter-McLemore is currently imprisoned for cultivating Cannabis for his severe and chronic depression and unstable appetite.

Dana C. (Florida) is 47 and she suffers from chronic back pain, digestive problems, and insomnia. She smokes Cannabis to relieve these ailments, but prefers to use a tincture when she can afford it.

Ashley C. (Georgia) is 45. He has bone spurs impinging on his spinal chord. He smokes Cannabis so that he can move his arms and hands.

Lonnie C. (Georgia) is 33 and has suffered from glaucoma since he was a teenager. In 1995 he received multiple injuries in a car accident. He was prescribed numerous drugs but none relieved his suffering. He employs Cannabis as often as he can afford, as it helps his pain and his mental clarity.

Kelly C. (Arizona) is 26. He is a hemophiliac with AIDS who contracted HIV at age nine through a blood transfusion. "If I don't have Cannabis, I'm incapable of eating, my nausea is so strong. Nothing else gives me any appetite at all."

Denise D. (Florida) is 37. She is anorexic and has bipolar disorder and schizophrenic tendencies. Smoking one Cannabis cigarette a day prevents drastic mood swings and stimulates her appetite. Without this medication, she has "psychotic breaks" from reality.

Rich E. (California) employs Cannabis for chronic depression.

Deborah F. (F) is 42. She has pain from MS and keratoconus. With Cannabis, she is more alert. She is allergic to conventional drugs.

Daniel F. (Ohio) is 37. He was hit by a train 1987 and is a paraplegic. The wide range of drugs he was prescribed hardly helped and he suffered debilitating and dangerous side effects, including addiction. Now, Daniel uses small amounts of Cannabis for his pain, to increase his appetite and help him to be productive.

Christopher F. (Kentucky) is only 18 years old. He was diagnosed with Oppositional Defiant Disorder, manic-depressive disorder, and Attitudinal Deficit Hyperactivity Disorder (ADHD). He needs Cannabis to control his violent mood-swings and to treat his depression. Teachers, surprised by his remarkable improvement, inquired into the cause. When he admitted his use of medical Cannabis, he was expelled; he is now forced to rely on home schooling.

William F. (Oklahoma) is 38 and is a U.S. Veteran. He has rheumatoid arthritis. He is also the father of three children. He was sentenced to 93 years for cultivation of Cannabis. (He was released after 5 years.)

Richard F. (Arizona) is 35 and has fibromyalgia. Prescription pain-killers don't help him, ""without Cannabis the pain is intolerable. I could not survive."

Lanny G. (North Carolina) is 47 and a U.S. veteran who suffers from PTSD and chronic pain from a shoulder injury. He uses Cannabis for relief of pain and cramping without the side effects of conventional medications.

Richard G. (North Carolina) is 40 and suffers from degenerative bone disease, arthritis, diabetes, fibromyalgia, manic depression, sleep disorders, and heart disease. Conventional medications aggravate his symptoms, while Cannabis provides serenity, sleep and emotional stability.

Tim H. (Arizona) is 49 and has had unexplained seizures his entire life. In 1996, after a massive cerebral hemorrhage, he was found to have a congenital arterio-vascular malformation. Anti-seizure medication hurt his digestive system. Cannabis alleviates his pain, calms his nerves and stomach and prevents seizures.

Joseph H. (Florida) is 49 and has AIDS. He credits his ten year record of health to his use of Cannabis for appetite, digestion, and stress reduction. "Marijuana kills stress and stress is very lethal for people with AIDS."

Dr. Andrew H. (Massachusetts) is a 39-year-old Multiple Sclerosis patient confined to a wheelchair. Upon reaching the tolerance level of his steroid medication, he began smoking Cannabis every other day to relax his muscles and to decrease his chronic pain.

Roy H. (Florida) is a 40-year-old U.S. Veteran and AIDS victim. Roy began using Cannabis for the effects of AZT and other AIDS inhibitors. He employs Cannabis to suppress his nausea, relax his cramps, alleviate his depression, stimulate his appetite, and to restore his energy.

Ladd H. (Iowa) is 47. He has MS and was approved for Cannabis Medicine under the Federal government's Compassionate IND program. The final forms were not processed, however, before the program was closed. He buys Cannabis illegally. It works to relieve his constant pain and to stop his muscle spasms.

Jodi J. (Florida) is 29 and has chronic pain from a back injury. Drugs left her sedated and bedridden. After 14 months, she stopped the drugs and switched to Cannabis. Now pregnant with her second child, she employs Cannabis to ease her back pain and to suppress nausea without feeling sedated.

Laura J. (Tennessee) is 41. She was diagnosed with episodic ataxia – a rare form of spino-cerebellum ataxia (SCA). She also suffers from imbalance, blurred vision, nausea, and muscle spasms. Laura switched to Cannabis after 20 years and feels no pain or nausea and can walk again.

Robert K. (Oregon) is 54. He fractured a vertebra and has severe digestive problems. He can block the pain, increase his concentration, and induce sleep with the aid of Cannabis. When confined to prescribed medications, he was constantly sedated and he suffered additional health risks due to side effects.

Dean K. is 35 and has AIDS. He employs Cannabis therapeutically for the past ten years to avoid stress induced HIV-related illness. Now that he must use aggressive AIDS medications, Cannabis allows him to suppress nausea, have an appetite and combat his depression.

John K. (Pennsylvania) is 29. He suffers from PTSD and also is diagnosed as a manic-depressive. A former drug and alcohol addict, he began to medicate himself with Cannabis to control his mood swings and was able to quit alcohol, as well.

Bryan K. (New Mexico) is 34 and is a psychiatric nurse (R.N.) He is fighting severe depression. Cannabis increases his appetite and motivates him to get up in the morning.

Robert K. (Florida) is 75. He was a long-term cigarette smoker and now employs Cannabis for the respiratory problem of COPD. "Cannabis is a natural bronchodilator. It opens my lungs and gives me life."

Kiyoshi K. (Pennsylvania) is 52 and has AIDS. He needs Cannabis to combat weight loss, as well as to reduce the nausea caused by HIV therapy.

Dennis L. (Vermont) is 49 and has Crohn's Disease. He uses Cannabis to ease his digestive problems and to relieve his chronic back pain.

Kay Lee (52) has Seasonal Affective Disorder, arthritis, and manic depression. She smokes Cannabis to reduce pain, induce sleep, and stimulate her appetite and to alleviate her depressive symptoms.

Jamie L. (Florida) is 27 and is an AIDS patient. He smokes Cannabis to fight dizziness, nausea, lethargy, seizures and depression. Arrested and beaten by police at a local Cannabis Buyer's Club in 1996, Jamie was awarded the right to use Cannabis therapeutically from the Florida Court. He intends to keep fighting until all patients are equally protected.

Arthur L. (Oregon) is 49 and suffers from bipolar affective disorder and uses Cannabis to control his mood swings. Arrested for growing Cannabis for personal medication, he is currently on probation.

Marshall L. (California) is 43 and is a paraplegic due to an automobile accident. "Conventional drugs used for spasticity put me in a stupor. "Cannabis relieves the spasms and the pain and I can function and it elevates my moods as well."

Tylan M. (Washington) is 39. He has permanent liver damage as a result of alcoholism. Told he would die, if he did not quit, he began smoking Cannabis. He has been arrested twice for marijuana possession, but continues to smoke it, "so I can eat and just be able to live."

James M. (Nevada) is 39 and employs Cannabis to stimulate his appetite, combat nausea and counter the wasting syndrome caused by the medication he is given to fight AIDS.

John M. (North Carolina) is 38. He has rheumatoid arthritis, depression, and insomnia. With prescribed medicines: "I would be very irritable and violent, as the chemicals built up in my system. The pills made me an angry hermit. I gave up the pills. Now I just use Cannabis and I feel calm and pain free."

Todd M. (California) is 26. He had cancer and many cancer treatments as a child resulting in dystrophic skeleton-muscular problems, such as spinal fusion, nerve damage and lumbar-scoliosis. Chemotherapy and radiation caused severe nausea and weight loss. Operations on his spine caused constant pain. Cannabis helps him to recover his appetite and reduce his considerable pain. He was arrested and imprisoned for 5 years by the federal government for growing marijuana.

Johanna M. (Washington) suffers from herniated discs and epilepsy. She takes Cannabis to help divert her attention from the severe pain. She founded Green Cross Patient Co-op in Washington to distribute marijuana to patients.

Peter M. (California) is 48 and has non-Hodgkin's lymphoma and HIV. He says, "I am alive today because of science and one ancient herb."

Robert, M. (Vermont) is 49 and is a Molecular Biology Professor. He has severe arthritis and a compressed fracture of the spine. He takes no prescription drugs, employing only Cannabis and a chiropractor to relieve his pain.

Robert M. (Arkansas) is 64. He has MS and employs Cannabis for imbalance, weakness, spasticity and low energy.

Debby M. (Kansas) is 49. She has insomnia and needs Cannabis to sleep and also as a stress reducer, and appetite stimulant. Arrested and placed on probation, she is fighting felony charges that could imprison her for life.

Johann M. (New York) is 35. He has Chronic Fatigue Immune Dysfunction and chronic candidiasis. He is sensitive to all chemicals. He employs Cannabis for gastrointestinal problems, pain, and for heightened energy.

Sister Somayah (California) is 47. She has Sickle Cell Anemia and is a U.S. veteran. She has constant flu-like symptoms, severe pain, nausea and dehydration. She needs Cannabis to live: "Without Cannabis I would die."

Barbara M. (Florida) had a massive heart attack. She cannot take prescription medication. She needs Cannabis for chronic back pain and for relief of stress.

Leonard M. (Idaho) is 58 and a U.S. Veteran with chronic pain and insomnia. He smokes Cannabis as a pain reliever and sleep aid. He wants Cannabis available by prescription so that he need not break the law.

Myron M. (California) is 35. He has diabetes that caused blindness. He also suffers from a paralyzed stomach and uncontrollable vomiting. Only Cannabis settles his nervous stomach and gives him an appetite.

Mitchell M. (California) is 40. He has chronic bronchitis, asthma, severe neck and lower spine deformities. Prescribed drugs almost killed him. Cannabis soothes his violent moods and eases his pain and helps to prevent asthma attacks.

Larry N. (Florida) is 47. He has an impacted vertebrae and scoliosis of the spine. He also suffers from arthritis. He needs Cannabis to reduce his pain. He is currently facing imprisonment for cultivation.

Michael O. (Washington) is a Viet Nam Veteran. He employs Cannabis for the symptoms of Delayed Stress Disorder.

Douglas P. (Georgia) is 18 and a University student. He suffers from astigmatism and eating disorders. Cannabis has helped to maintain his weight by stimulating his appetite and eliminating his nausea. His astigmatism also seems to be helped with Cannabis.

Daryl P (Minnesota) is 26. He has spasticity, nausea, and depression caused by Cerebral Palsy. Wheelchair-bound, conventional medications aggravate his nausea and add to his stress. Cannabis allows him to eat. It calms his anxiety and depression.

Mac P. (Nevada) is 33. He has AIDS and is prescribed Marinol. He says: "I kept throwing the pills up. Stress is my enemy. Cannabis works like a charm. No more nausea and I feel calm."

Ror P. (Colorado) is 50. He has MS and has had four colostomies. Taking Prednisone caused extreme bloating and irritability. "The odor from the external colostomy ruined my appetite. My physician states that Cannabis helps me for all my problems - including my loss of appetite."

John P. (Ohio) is 33. He needs Cannabis to fight the pain, dizziness, spacticity weight loss and nausea associated with MS. He is an activist and has testified before the Ohio State Legislature.

Robin P. (Montana) is 40. She has Lupus and suffers from migraines, fibromyalgia, degenerative disc damage, nausea, and chronic pain. When prescribed medications had no effect on her symptoms, she researched treatment options and began smoking Cannabis to combat her symptoms. Now able to function, she fights for the right to obtain Cannabis legally.

Don R. (New Jersey) is 52. He has Chronic Fatigue Syndrome and takes Cannabis to heighten his focus and to reduce discomfort caused by muscle weakness and cramping.

Kenneth R. (Ohio) is 42. He has MS and is a U.S. Veteran. He needs Cannabis to combat severe spasticity and to restore his balance. He had no success with conventional medication. "Cannabis makes me feel normal."

Jackie R. (Wisconsin) is 46. She has Ehler's Danlos syndrome, a degenerative· disease ·of elastic connective tissue. She uses Cannabis to reduce chronic joint pain and as an appetite stimulant. After being approved for the federal government's Compassionate IND program, the program was shut down and she never received her medicine.

Ralph R. (Ohio) suffered an accident that severed the cartilage in his knees, fractured his shoulder, and caused a bulging vertebral disc in his neck. He also suffers from PTSD. His prescribed medicine caused organ damage. Now he substitutes Cannabis for nausea, vomiting, depression, and anxiety attacks and also as a pain remedy. His doctors have recommended Cannabis. He must keep it a secret to avoid losing his Social Security and medical benefits.

John R. (Alaska) is 51. He has non-Hodgkin's Lymphoma from Agent Orange while a Marine in Vietnam. Arrested by federal agents for growing Cannabis in his home, he was under home detention because of his disease. "I fought for the ideal of liberty. Shouldn't that include choice of medicine?"

Scott R. (Maryland) is 50 and a veteran who suffers from PTSD, a fractured skull, severe knee injuries and exposure to Agent Orange. "Only Cannabis helps."

Donna R. (Florida) is 44 and has epilepsy, had a stroke, suffers migraines, arthritis, and a detached retina. Cannabis allows her to breathe normally, control her seizures and migraines and reduce arthritic pain and lower the pressure In her eyes. "It is a god-send."

Richard S. (Delaware) is 46. He has glaucoma, bone spurs and chromic back pain with muscle spasms. He suffered adverse reactions to prescribed steroids. Richard acted on a doctor's suggestion that Cannabis might relieve his symptoms, "which it does!'

Elise S. (Pennsylvania) is 46. She had asthma 30 years ago. She always smoked Cannabis recreationally. When she stopped using Cannabis when she was 44 for a brief time, she developed MS. "I always had MS, according to the doctors, I just didn't know it because I smoked marijuana regularly." Without Cannabis, she cannot function. "Marijuana has saved my life."

Lynette S. (California) is 44. She suffers from toxic pollution. Only Cannabis helps her to breathe and to relieve her depression.

Ron S. (Michigan) is 49. He suffers from post-polio syndrome and spinal cord atrophy. His doctors will allow a morphine pump implanted in his stomach. He would prefer to smoke Cannabis to control intense muscle spasms and pain rather than undergo unnecessary surgery and endure the side effects of morphine.

Kim S. (North Carolina) is 39. She has Herpes with associated "breakouts," expressed in rashes, nervousness and agitation. While other medications were ineffective, Cannabis has decreased the breakouts, and reduced her stress levels without side effects.

Dr. Richard S. (Florida) is 46. He has Attention Deficit Disorder and was prescribed Ritalin and other medications to counter his lack of concentration. He switched to Cannabis because of the ineffectiveness of drugs. Marinol is helpful, but the cost is too great. He buys Cannabis on the black market and fears that he will be arrested. "It works very well."

BDS is a 15-year-old who employs Cannabis for chronic headaches and nausea caused by a brain lesion in the area of his pineal gland.

Greta S. (Louisiana) is 30. She has Wilson's Disease. She needs Cannabis because her body cannot eliminate copper. "My larynx was completely paralyzed. The doctors could not help. I couldn't speak for over 2 years. I tried Cannabis for 7 days and then my voice began to return. "Without Cannabis, I could not talk.

Denise S. (Pennsylvania) is 35. She has AIDS. She needs Cannabis to fight the nausea and dizziness of her treatment.

Katrina S. (Texas) is 39. She had gastric bypass to control her obesity. An implant was forgotten in her abdomen during the operation. Now she has violent intestinal contractions, unbearable headaches, a hernia and she vomits blood. She is wheelchair-bound. She needs Cannabis for all her problems. "Simple, otherwise, I die."

Roy S. (Florida) has bipolar disorder. Cannabis regulates his mood swings and eases his chronic pain.

C.T. (Vermont) is 20 and has had at least one violent epileptic seizure every day since he was 13. Drugs don't work. He must be monitored constantly. But with Cannabis, there are no seizures at all.

Joe T. (Florida) is 44. He has chronic pain from a fractured back. He treats his pain with Cannabis instead of addictive drugs, which caused him severe gastro-intestinal problems.

Pebbles T. (California) is 54 and has severe migraines and needs Cannabis to reduce both the frequency and severity of her headaches. She has been arrested four times on Cannabis charges and is currently appealing her conviction based on the California Medical Marijuana Law.

Lori V. (Vermont) is 46. She has a bad back injury, severe migraine headaches, arthritis and a sleep disorder. Cannabis is effective and safer than the prescribed drugs that made her sleep all the time.

Susan V. (California) is 35. Her breast implants ruptured. She has cancer of the breast. After breast surgery, she developed chronic muscle pain, nausea, and weight loss. "Cannabis relieves me of all these symptoms."

Dan W. (North Carolina) is 36. Dan needs Cannabis to ease the chronic pain in his edemic leg and ankle.

Lennice W (Virginia) is 46. She has fits of manic rage, nervousness and depression. She tried prescription medicines to no avail. Although she deplores breaking the law, she uses Cannabis, because it is the only medicine that is effective.

Casey W. (Washington) is 34. He has AIDS and a fragile liver from hepatitis. He cannot take AIDS-inhibitor medications. Casey began smoking Cannabis when told he would die. It helps his nausea, weakness, depression, and insomnia. After 6 years, he feels healthy and says his medicinal choice of Cannabis set him on the path to health.

Jess W (Washington) is 50 and he uses Cannabis to combat depression and heart disease.

John W. (Texas) is 42. He suffers from severe bipolar syndrome. Prescribed drugs made his symptoms so exaggerated that he became nearly catatonic. He eats two grams of Cannabis every morning and smokes a few puffs in the afternoon. "I don't feel high, just normal."

Notes:

CPSIA information can be obtained at www.ICGtesting.com
Printed in the USA
BVOW031056280212

284003BV00012B/53/P